PENGUIN CLASSICS

YUSUF'S FRAGRANCE

Mahmud Gāmi stands out among the Kashmiri poets as a pioneer in introducing the Persian genres of the *ghazal, nazm, masnavi* and *nāt* into Kashmiri. Not only is he the first truly prolific poet of the language, but much of his poetry is also remarkable for its beauty of expression and depth of thought. His *vatsuns* (lyrical poems) and *masnavis* (narrative poems) such as 'Yusuf Zulaykha', 'Khusrau Shīrīn', 'Layla Majnun' and 'Sheikh San'ān' have rightly been acclaimed as significant contributions to Kashmiri poetry.

Born and raised in Srinagar, **Mufti Mudasir Farooqi** is a faculty member of the Department of English, University of Kashmir. Proficient in English, Kashmiri, Urdu, Persian and Arabic, he has made academic contributions to several areas such as literary theory and criticism, postmodern drama, Kashmir history and literature, Indo-Persian literature and Islamic studies. He was a postdoctoral fellow in the research programme 'Future Philology: Revisiting the Canons of Textual Scholarship' at Freie University of Berlin in 2012–13.

His English translation of Kashmir's foremost Persian poet Tahir Ghani Kashmiri *The Captured Gazelle: The Poems of Ghani Kashmiri* was published as a Penguin Classic in 2013 while an annotated Urdu translation of Ghani's complete works titled *Aatash-e Toor: Deewan-e Ghani Kashmiri* has come out in 2022. *Yusuf's Fragrance* is his fourth book.

Yusuf's Fragrance
Poems of Mahmud Gāmi

MAHMUD GĀMI

Translated by Mufti Mudasir Farooqi

PENGUIN BOOKS

An imprint of Penguin Random House

PENGUIN BOOKS

USA | Canada | UK | Ireland | Australia
New Zealand | India | South Africa | China | Singapore

Penguin Books is part of the Penguin Random House group of companies
whose addresses can be found at global.penguinrandomhouse.com

Published by Penguin Random House India Pvt. Ltd
4th Floor, Capital Tower 1, MG Road,
Gurugram 122 002, Haryana, India

First published in Penguin Books by Penguin Random House India 2022

10 9 8 7 6 5 4 3 2

ISBN 9780143452713

Typeset in Sabon by Manipal Technologies Limited, Manipal

Printed at Repro India Limited

www.penguin.co.in

This is a legitimate digitally printed version of the book and therefore might not
have certain extra finishing on the cover.

For my son,
Mufti Khaleed Farooqi

Contents

~

Foreword

~

The very decision of choosing Mahmud Gāmi for translation out of a host of Sufi poets of Kashmir expresses Professor Mufti Mudasir's critical estimate of the whole gamut of mystic poetry, especially Kashmiri Sufi poetry. Every good act of translation, first of all, involves an exercise of options. Out of a variety of options available to him, Professor Mufti Mudasir too had a long tradition spread over 700 years in his language in which many poets have excelled. The choice for Mahmud Gāmi's lyrics and narrative poems abundantly reveals the translator's five types of competences: (i) his appreciation of the universals of poetry, (ii) his thorough knowledge of all other Sufi poets in the language, (iii) his comparative method of appreciation, (iv) his critical appreciation in choosing one version out of several given versions of the same text and (v) his felicity in finding most satisfying English equivalents for the words and expressions peculiar of the Oriental Classical poetry. Putting his freedom of choice among the available options makes his English translation of Mahmud Gāmi's works easily available to readers who are interested in the works of the poet in particular, and the Classical poetry of the East in general.

Even a cursory reading of Professor Mufti Mudasir's English translation convinces me that he has read and availed himself of many of those translations of Persian literature in English that were accomplished by the all-time great Orientalists who enthusiastically engaged themselves in unravelling the treasures of Iranian literature. One of them was William Jones who discovered for the first time in 1786, the notion of common descent of all languages of Europe, India and Iran, called Proto-Indo-European and invited the Western readers to the fecund literature obtaining in these languages. William Jones, with a taste of the East, translated many works of the Iranian literature that took the readers in Europe by surprise.

Translations of the selected excerpts from Mahmud Gāmi's works sufficiently reveal the genius of the poet who, after Sheikh Nooruddin of the fifteenth century, emerged as the maker of modern Kashmiri literature, introducing various literary forms, variety of lexis, and multifarious, delightful aspects of the world around, and at the same time developed suitable lexis enriched by appropriate Persian and Arabic borrowings. The real strength of Mahmud Gāmi's poetry is his swaying lyricism, impossible to transfer to any other text, within the language or in any other language, yet Mufti Mudasir conveys the beauty of feeling and equivalent imagery in English that has its own standards of music and verbal expression.

The translation has many more merits that demand greater length for appreciation than this brief note. I wish him great success.

Shafi Shauq
Chandpura, Harvan
February 2022

INTRODUCTION

~

Life

Mahmud Gāmi occupies a very prominent place in Kashmir's literary tradition and is rightly considered a towering figure. His contribution to Kashmiri poetry is unique both in its scope and depth. Not only is he the first truly prolific poet of Kashmiri, but much of his poetry also stands out for its beauty of expression and depth of thought—touchstones by which we generally measure a poet's value.

Born in 1765 in a village called Aadveder in Shahabad, south Kashmir, now renamed Mahmudabad after him, he lived a long life and died there in 1855. There is sufficient evidence to suggest that Gāmi was quite popular even during his lifetime. Waliyullah Mattoo (d. 1858), his contemporary, himself a poet and chronicler of note, pays tribute to Gāmi in his narrative poem 'Hīmāl':

> Among the Kashmiris especially well known
> Is Mahmud Gāmi, lesser than none
> From Shahabad, who has rejoiced my heart
> A master craftsman of Kashmiri verse
> Many nights have I spent savouring his honey
> I found him unique, peerless.[1]

Gāmi's poems were quite popular throughout Kashmir. They were not only transmitted orally but also copied extensively, as a large number of manuscripts of his poetry still found in different parts of Kashmir testify. His immense popularity during his lifetime and afterwards secured him a firm place in the public imaginary. Though still popular today, Gāmi has remained largely critically neglected.[2]

Gāmi's real name was Mahmud Shah. He adopted the penname Gāmi to rhyme with Nizāmi (1141–1209) and Jāmi (1414–1492), the two great classical Persian poets and his literary models; not, as some have speculated, as a proud marker of his identity as a villager because some city snobs had derided him as a *gāmi* (villager). Anecdotes abound about how Gāmi began writing poetry, all of which have little historical validity.[3] Gāmi must have received religious education at home and the local *madrasa* according to the norm of the day, giving him a basic knowledge of Arabic and Persian. That he knew Persian well and also wrote poems in it is beyond doubt. In fact, it is very probable that he began to versify in Persian before turning to Kashmiri. According to some sources, in his early years he earned his living as a teacher. Later in life, he became a popular village *pir*, a highly respected man sought by people for guidance in religious and spiritual matters.

One of Gāmi's sons, Shah Sultan died young and Gāmi grieved his loss in a moving elegy which contains the following lines:

May I be your sacrifice!
Shah Sultan, my dearest one
May I lay down my life for you!
Show me a single glimpse of yours.

Why have you spilled my blood
And dyed your feet and hands with it?
Could my blood fetch me your talking again!
O my sweet-lipped darling!

I don't know how I will die
Perhaps pining sorely for you!
How much more will Mahmud bear
This pain, this agony?
O dear one
May I be your sacrifice!

Gāmi was born during the Afghan rule (1749–1819) and died in 1855, a few years after the Dogras had taken over Kashmir following the infamous Treaty of Amritsar in 1846. He thus witnessed three regimes during his lifetime, including the Sikh rule (1820–1846), but much like most poets of his age, there is next to nothing in his poetry related to the social or political conditions of his times. In Gāmi's entire corpus, there is perhaps only one instance where a contemporary event of significance is dealt with: an elegiac poem written on the death of Abdullah Khan Alkozay, an Afghan Governor of Kashmir (1796–1806), whom he praises highly for his justice and kindness.[4] A few verses from the elegy go like this:

His mother cried from the women's chamber
'Oh, what shall I say, what shall I say!
O Abdullah Khan, why have you left
in the prime of your youth?'

A golden palanquin with hanging pearls
awaits you in vain
O graceful youth how many pearl-decked maidens
have you left scarred![5]

Hurry up, go out to dispense justice
to the people waiting outside.
O lion roaring in his den!
O Anushirvan, listen to the pleas of the oppressed![6]

An ardent Muslim, you did not
make merry like the god Indra
Alas, we did not prize your life enough!
Day and night you immersed yourself
in reciting the Quran
O Abdullah Khan, why have you left
in the prime of your youth?

God's creation was pleased with you,
Food grains were cheap and plentiful.
O Abdullah Khan, why have you left
in the prime of your youth?

Had I time enough,
I would say much more
of you and your noble deeds.
Still, this much I say: the year was
twelve hundred and twenty-one.[7]

To whom will Mahmud relate
this heart-wrenching tale?
O Abdullah Khan, why have you left
in the prime of your youth?

A telling piece of evidence of Gāmi's popularity in the late 19th century is that Karl Friedrich Buckhardt, a German Orientalist who was in Kashmir in the last quarter of that century, found him a household name and decided to translate a major portion of his *masnavi* (long narrative poem in rhyming couplets) 'Yusuf Zulaykha' into Latin with the help of some natives.[8] Unfortunately, nothing else is known about Gāmi's life.

That Gāmi was deeply religious is borne out by his poetry very clearly. His worldview is profoundly mystical and his lyrical and narrative poems are directly inspired by religious ideas. He is also the first poet of Kashmiri to have left a popular corpus of *nāts*, that is, poems written in praise of the Prophet Muhammad. A *nāt* beginning with the following lines indicates Gāmi's formative influence on the subsequent *nāt* poets of Kashmiri:

> Banish my grief, O living Prophet!
> Give me a cure, O living Prophet!
> The verse, 'By the night', extols your hair
> And 'By the bright morn', alludes to your shining face.[9]

He draws profusely from the Islamic tradition, using episodes and stories of the prominent figures of Islamic history, including the Prophet and his family. A short narrative poem titled 'Yak Hikāyat' (A Story), relates how the Prophet was found missing by his family and friends one night and traced only after a long and frantic search in a graveyard—where he was discovered praying earnestly to God to forgive his people. Another poem 'Mirāj Nāmah' (The Tale of Ascension) describes the Prophet's journey to the heavens, and yet another describes the death of his daughter Fātima very poignantly.

Critical Reception

Mahmud Gāmi is, by critical consensus, considered a pioneer in introducing the Persian genres such as *ghazal*, *nazm*, *masnavi* and *nāt* into Kashmiri. M.Y. Taing, a noted critic, remarks that Gāmi took Kashmiri to a new level of accomplishment by making it a robust literary language. For a couple of centuries before Gāmi, Kashmiri poetry had little to boast of and folksongs had become its most common literary expression. For Taing, Gāmi restored to Kashmiri the depth and scope it possessed in a bygone age, best represented in the genius of Lalla Ded (1320–1392). Taing also uses the epithet 'a great language-fashioning poet' for Gāmi. After Gāmi, the Kashmiri poetic tradition progressed quickly and produced great names like Maqbool Krālwāri, Rasul Mir, Parmanand, Prakash Ram and countless others.[10]

Some literary scholars think that Kashmiri poetry must have begun a long time before Lalla Ded because her poems suggest a literary tradition fully matured and not one in an incipient stage.[11] If this is true, whatever there was before Lalla is irretrievably lost. Not only this, the extant Kashmiri poetry from Lalla to Gāmi is scant and intermittent. Barring a few famous poets such as Lalla herself, Sheikh Nuruddin (1377–1440) and Habba Khatoon, the Kashmiri literary landscape before Gāmi wore an impoverished look. With these few exceptions, the poetic tradition that he inherited was enervated. It is into this lacklustre tradition that Gāmi tried to infuse a new life. It is, therefore, not surprising that Abdul Ahad Āzād, who is also the first literary historian of Kashmiri, calls him the Rudaki of Kashmiri poetry, and Taing invokes the names of both Rudaki and Chaucer to place him in the Kashmiri poetic tradition.[12]

What Taing observes is reinforced by Shafi Shauq, a noted scholar of Kashmiri, whose estimate, even if a little exaggerated, sums up Gāmi's contribution to Kashmiri poetry:

> The history of the last two hundred years of Kashmiri poetry is, in essence, a struggle by our poets to emerge from the overwhelming influence of Mahmud Gami. Mahmud chose a particular course within Kashmiri poetry, opted for a certain manner of expression, and kept widening his domain till he cultivated a unique style of his own. He perfected this style so that its full potential was realised. Doing so, he left his successors no option but to retell what he had already said.[13]

Gāmi, by Shauq's evaluation, laid down the course, defined the limits and determined the style and content for his successors and they had no option but to follow him.[14] Gāmi's influence on his successors such as Rasul Mir can be a fascinating subject for research. Perhaps some anecdotes originating in the countryside which bring together Gāmi and Rasul Mir in a single story, with the former making certain predictions about the latter, point to how Rasul Mir was seen as the rightful successor of Gāmi in popular imagination. According to an anecdote, Gāmi met young Rasul Mir and, after gauging him, exclaimed, '*ames chi jāne margi hind karen!*', an expression with an equivocal meaning: (a) this young man holds an exceptional promise; or (b) this man will die young.[15] The words proved prophetic as both the meanings came true. Mir died young but only after he had made his mark as an exceptionally good poet. A cursory look at Rasul Mir's work reveals many thematic and stylistics debts to Gāmi. A closer look can bring out many aspects of this poetic influence.

While Rasul Mir emulated and perhaps even excelled Gāmi in lyrical poetry, he did not attempt other forms, especially the *masnavi*. Similarly, although Maqbool Shah Krālwāri wrote 'Gulrez', perhaps the artistically most consummate *masnavi* in Kashmiri, he did not make a similar mark in lyrical poetry. Gāmi thus stands alone as a trendsetter in multiple genres of Kashmiri poetry.

Gāmi and the Persian Influence

Persian, a cosmopolitan language that enjoyed high prestige in the Indian subcontinent for well over six centuries, had a prominent place in Kashmir too, from the time of the Shahmiri rule (1339–1561) up to the end of the 19th century, when it began to lose its prominence. The influence of Persian on vernacular Kashmiri has been immense. By the age of Gāmi, Kashmiri bore Persian's unmistakable mark, surpassing that of Sanskrit, which was the major source of its vocabulary in the pre-Islamic era and for some time after the advent of Islam. As Alexander Beecroft has noted, a vernacular literature can 'compete with, complement, or otherwise coexist with a cosmopolitan literary language', and also 'exist in symbiosis with it'.[16] One of the ways that a vernacular can announce this symbiosis is 'through emulation of major works of the cosmopolitan canon'.[17] Beecroft makes another insightful remark, in the European context, regarding Lithuanian, a vernacular, and Latin, a cosmopolitan language, which is illuminating with regard to the relation of Kashmiri to Persian as well. Kashmiri, we may say, using Beecroft's insight, 'was never significantly in competition with' Persian, since by the time Kashmiri 'emerged as a genuinely viable literary option', Persian had 'ceased to be a major structuring feature of the literary ecology' of Kashmir.[18]

Gāmi is the pioneer of a new literary form—translation–adaptation and is the first major poet–translator working between the cosmopolitan Persian and vernacular Kashmiri. Despite the resurgence of Kashmiri poetry in the late 18th century, Persian continued to enjoy official patronage for nearly a century, and Kashmiri poets drew profusely on Persian sources to breathe fresh life into the vernacular literature. There is nothing to suggest that Persian was viewed as an alien language by Kashmiri litterateurs and that those who preferred Kashmiri to Persian did it to challenge its supremacy.

The notion, created by some literary historians and critics, that Kashmiri poets writing in the 18th and 19th centuries were making attempts, albeit half-heartedly, to break free from the influence of Persian is an erroneous one. As an example, we can sense an unwarranted anxiety—stemming perhaps from the rise of the new Kashmiri nationalist consciousness to which he contributed at the time—informing Abdul Ahad Āzād's literary history *Kashmiri Zabān aur Shāyri* (1959), a work in three volumes. He denounces what he sees as a stifling influence of Persian on Kashmiri and regrets that the latter took too long to break free from this influence and come of age. His history is replete with diatribes against the 'imitation of Persian' by Kashmiri poets.[19] Āzād's nationalist-oriented literary history is marred by the underlying notion of 'contamination' of Kashmiri poetry by 'foreign' influences, especially Persian. All through his treatment of the problem, Āzād betrays a poor understanding of the multiple ways in which a cosmopolitan language can enrich a vernacular. Another notable Kashmiri scholar, J.L. Kaul, though more guarded than Āzād, still laments the Kashmiri poets' turning 'to old Persian themes of legend and story, to Shirin and Farhad, Laila and Majnoon, Wamiq and Uzra, Sohrab'.[20]

The fact, however, is that far from being a constricting and thus a baneful influence, Persian enormously enriched Kashmiri in more ways than one. Not only did Persian provide Kashmiri with a hitherto unavailable repertoire of symbols, metaphors and similes, but also made it thematically more versatile and richer. One can only imagine how impoverished Kashmiri poetry would have been without the Persian influence with its vast resource of vocabulary, literary devices, genres and themes which together came to constitute the warp and woof of Kashmiri poetry.

The notion that Kashmiri poetry came of age insofar as it successfully broke from the overriding Persian literary influence, therefore, must be rejected. Not only did Kashmiri poetry enrich itself through this appropriation, but it also enabled its readers an entrance and imaginative participation into a larger and richer literary tradition.

This is not to suggest that translation–adaptation should be seen as an ideologically neutral enterprise or that the texts so produced did not contribute to strengthening the self-perception of the Kashmiri Muslims as part of a larger religious community spread over the Persianate world and beyond. In fact, the very choice of particular texts and not others, for translation is an ideologically fraught exercise.[21] The notion—repeated tirelessly in discussions and writings on Kashmir—of a Kashmiri identity transcending religious affiliations and inscribed in the aesthetics of mystical and love poetry of the land is superficial at best.[22]

Gāmi's conscious borrowing from the Persian masters signals the extent to which a major Kashmiri poetic voice was ready to appropriate the Persian literary tradition, thus 'announcing a symbiosis through emulation'. He wrote lyrics, narrative romances and devotional poems in praise of the Prophet Muhammad and thus gave Kashmiri an impetus it badly needed. His oft-repeated invocation of Nizāmi and Jāmi towards the end of his *masnavis* suggests that he aspired to be placed among the great masters of Persian verse and saw his Kashmiri adaptations as a continuity of, rather than a break from, the Persian tradition.

> Countless blessings of God be on Nizāmi
> A servant at his door is Mahmud Gāmi

or:

> Jāmi had told this tale of Zulaykha
> Gāmi says the same in Kashmiri

Again, in a *nāt* Gāmi writes:

> Nizāmi sings your praise
> Jāmi extols your virtues
> What more can Gāmi say?
> O God's messenger, blessings on you!

With him a barren period of Kashmiri poetry came to an end and the language witnessed an extraordinary flourishing of poetry in many genres. Gāmi's decision to choose Kashmiri instead of Persian for his poetic expression proved to be a momentous one as it served as a model and inspiration for future poets. Interestingly, there is hardly any mention of any Kashmiri poet by Gāmi, while Persian poets like Nizāmi, Attār, Rumi and Jāmi are mentioned often. What explains Gāmi's decision to draw prodigiously from the Persian literary sources was, partly at least, the near absence of a rich surviving poetic heritage in Kashmiri.

Philosophy of Love

Kashmiri Sufi poets have subscribed to the doctrine of the 'transcendent unity of being' called *wahdatul wujood*. The doctrine first found a systematic treatment in the works of the Spanish Muslim Sufi and thinker Ibn Arabi (1165–1240) known throughout the Islamic world as Great Master (Sheikh-e Akbar). For all the complexity and controversy it has raised, the doctrine became immensely popular with Persian poets and was also appropriated by many theologians and incorporated into an Islamic paradigm. For its proponents, *wahdatul wujood* is not pantheistic or even panentheistic. In the words of S.H. Nasr, while 'pantheism implies a substantial continuity between God and the Universe', Ibn Arabi claims, 'God's absolute transcendence over every category, including that of substance'.[23] The doctrine, therefore, does not imply God's identification with the Universe: 'It means, rather, that while God is absolutely transcendent with respect to the Universe, the Universe is not completely separated from Him; that the Universe is mysteriously plunged in God.'[24]

According to Ibn Arabi, the Universe is 'divine-disclosure', a manifestation of divine names and attributes. The reason why the Universe came to be in the first place was the desire of the Eternal Being to manifest Himself. The following words, attributed to the Prophet of Islam by some Sufis but certainly not authentic, sum up how the riddle of existence was explained: 'The Almighty God says, "I was a hidden treasure and desired to be known, so I created the creation."' Since Ibn Arabi sees the world as the manifestation of God's names and attributes, only insofar as He has revealed Himself through them can He be known. All things derive their existence from God and the world is but a dim reflection of His infinite attributes. The world is therefore a theophany—God's self-revelation. Persian poets largely adopted the doctrine of Ibn Arabi and it subsequently found its way into other literary traditions where Persian was a major influence. Though Ibn Arabi's doctrine spread far and wide, it was through the poetry of Jāmi that *wahdatul wujood* became quite popular with the poets of the Indian subcontinent. William Chittick has rightly pointed out that a major reason for the spread of Ibn Arabi's school in the Indian subcontinent was the great popularity of Jāmi's writings in the region.[25]

Referring to the Quranic verse where God addresses Satan after his refusal to prostrate before Adam, 'What prevented you (Satan) from prostrating yourself to him whom I have created with my own hands' (38:75), Jāmi interprets two hands as two categories of divine attributes: the attributes of beauty (*jamāl*) and the attributes of majesty (*jalāl*). Only man, says Jāmi, was created by two hands, meaning that only man is the locus of manifestation of both beauty and majesty. Everything else was created only with one hand. Again, Jāmi in the prologue to his 'Yusuf and Zulaykha' provides the central theme of speculative

Sufism, according to which the divine is represented as a beautiful lady in her chamber. The lady 'is contemplating her beauty in the mirror of the Universe which owes its existence to no one but herself.'[26] Here is the passage in de Bruijn's translation:

> In private room where being had no sign
> The world was stored away in non-existence
>
> One being was, untouched by duplication
> Far beyond any talk of 'we' and 'you'
>
> A Beauty sat, detached from all appearance
> Visible only to herself by her own light
>
> A ravishing Beloved in seclusion,
> Her garment still unsoiled by imperfection
>
> No mirror held reflection from Her face
> No comb could pass its fingers through her ringlets
>
> No wind was able to unbind a single hair.
> Her eye had never seen the slightest make-up
>
> The love-songs that she heard were all her own
> No lover played with her but She alone
>
> However, as the beautiful are bound to
> She also could not suffer her seclusion

If this must be, wherever beauty dwells
Such urge arose from Eternal Beauty

She moved her tent outside the sacred bounds
Revealed Herself to souls and to horizons

A different face appeared in every mirror
Her being was discussed in every place[27]

This explains how the desire of self-manifestation became the cause of existence. Kashmiri Sufi poets embraced this idea wholeheartedly. Love for them, therefore, is a metaphysical principle and not merely a literary invention. In one his poems, Gāmi says, 'He is here to behold Himself' (*pānay pānas wuchnay aaw*). This opening line which is also the refrain in the poem clearly foregrounds the Sufi idea of 'Oneness' manifesting itself in multiple forms:

How shall man explain this oneness?
He is here to behold Himself.

Slowly this truth will dawn upon him
He is one, has countless names.
What can an ignorant one know of it?
He is here to behold Himself

The bazaar of beauty is on display
Priceless is every curve and cut.
You put a high price on my pearl
He is here to behold Himself[28]

Creation, which manifests God's names, is seen as a mirror in which God sees Himself. As Cyrus Zargar has pointed out, 'Creation is receptive and, like an uncluttered mirror, serves as the means for God to witness himself'. Throughout this process, creation is both seer and seen, and yet the actual seer and seen are God. Moreover, this 'seeing' or 'witnessing' is for Ibn Arabi 'the primary purpose of creation.'[29] In Gāmi's 'Yusuf Zulaykha', Yusuf explains this idea to Bibi Rābia, a woman enamoured of his beauty, in this way:

> God created countless spirits in the world
> Pure from blemish like spotless mirrors
>
> The 'hidden one' could not brook self-concealment
> He took a mirror and got engrossed in Himself
>
> You can see Him in lovely curls and dusky moles
> A single beauty manifests in myriad forms
>
> A million mirrors reflect Him alone
> Matter and spirit, within and without
>
> When face to face with an appearance
> Leave the husk, catch the kernel within
>
> Forms infinite have a single core
> In the beginning there was just one

Forms will decay, come what may
Fix your eyes on the meaning's core

Choose a love which will ever be yours
Love Him who will live eternally.

For Sufis, Man the microcosm and the Universe the
macrocosm, reflect each other as two mirrors facing
each other. In another poem titled 'Dard-e naystān'
(The Reed Bed's Pain), Gāmi dwells on the idea of
nothingness prior to the creation of the world and the
'I' that first brought everything else into being:

A musical note fell into my ears
I will sing of the reed bed's pain

God's throne was not yet built
He sat in an emptiness of vast expanse
There was no count of days or years
I will sing of the reed bed's pain

No rain fell, no crops grew
Chaos held sway everywhere
The 'Word' was unborn, the path unknown
I will sing of the reed bed's pain

Adam and Eve were uncreated yet
Only the almond orchard bloomed
No grain was eaten, no leaf fell on the ground
I will sing of the reed bed's pain

Alif and *meem* were joined together[30]
Then the mirror got sullied
Became hazy first, then befuddled
Letters *dāl*, *zāl*, *ray*, *zay* et al. had no existence
I will sing of the reed bed's pain

This prodigal sea has inebriated many
Reason and Intelligence stand wonderstruck
Essence manifested itself through Attributes
I will sing of the reed bed's pain

Mahmud bears witness to the coming of being
Being owes its existence to 'I'
'I AM' is what Mansur did proclaim
I will sing of the reed bed's pain[31]

The poem is strikingly reminiscent of the opening of Rumi's *masnavi* 'The Lament of the Reed Flute'. While in Rumi, the reed flute laments its tearing away from the reed bed and longs to reunite with it, Gāmi projects the lament on to the reedbed. In Gāmi, it is the reedbed which becomes a symbol of the Primordial Reality and the poem a threnody articulating its great yearning for self-manifestation. Again, while Rumi deals with the idea of separation from the point of view of the reedflute, Gāmi is tackling a deeper mystery: why did the separation take place at all? Making its way through a dense thicket of metaphors and mystical allusions, the poem provides an answer at the end—it is 'I', proclaimed so audaciously by

Mansur, though at his own peril—that holds the key
to the puzzle of being.

Major Themes: Love and Death

Shafi Shauq describes Gāmi as the founder of Sufi
poetry in Kashmiri.[32] Although this is largely a correct
description, the term Sufi or mystical is too limiting
to describe him. This is because, regardless of the fact
that much of his corpus deals with what we might
call earthly, romantic or profane love, even within the
broad category of the religious, Gāmi's poems cover
a wide range of themes—from the purely mystical
to devotional, doctrinal, meditative, homiletic and
eschatological.

An important point to bear in mind is the vital
distinction, brought out by Lowry Nelson in his
discussion of mystical poetry, between poetry
written *about* mystical ideas and poetry that aims to
communicate the experience itself.[33] Gāmi's poems,
as well as those of most other Kashmiri poets who
are classified as Sufi, fall in the former rather than
the latter category. Few of Gāmi's poems could be
described as examples of a direct experience of the
divine.

Some misunderstandings about Sufism, namely,
that it is so obsessed with the spiritual that it detests
everything physical or material; it values the esoteric
so much that the exoteric is seen merely as a shell
hiding the kernel; or it is implacably opposed to

pleasure of any kind, are quite widespread. Gāmi's poetry helps dispel these misconceptions. He celebrates love in all its forms, refusing to regard it exclusively as either spiritual or physical. Combining the physical with the spiritual, the intellectual with the emotional and the embodied with the ethereal is characteristic of Gāmi. A few examples will illustrate this point:

> He who was my life and soul
> left me crazed and fled.

> Lured me into a tavern
> made me drink cup after cup
> squeezed all soberness from me
> left me crazed and fled.

> He combed his locks straight
> and confounded the poor hyacinth.
> He, the lord of the fairy world,
> left me crazed and fled.[34]

~

> Where have you hidden yourself
> letting my garden's bloom go waste?
> Or are you enjoying a nap by a spring?
> Come, love, sit awhile.[35]

~

Away you stay from love's station
While longings surge within me.
I shall surely die this way.
This separation chips off my frame
And leaves me benumbed.
While your languid eyes torch me down.

Once we sat face to face
Held together by love's thrall
That is a vain craving now.
Waiting, my eyes have turned drowsy.
Why have you turned so unresponsive, cold?[36]

Gāmi's is, therefore, not a flesh-denying poetics. In his poems, he does not draw a sharp line between earthly and divine love. Amorous verses exist alongside penitential religious verses, and sometimes in a single poem the address shifts from the earthly beloved to God and vice versa. This, however, does not mean that Gāmi collapses the distinction between spirit and matter. For him, the physical or material world is subservient to the spiritual, and the function of poetry is to capture universal spiritual truths through a symbolic representation. The lover's state is emblematic of the soul in exile waiting ardently to return to its origin. The soul, according to the Sufi worldview, is essentially uncreated and partakes in divinity. Love is a power that pervades all creation, a strong attraction that not only exists in its most palpable form between a man and a woman but also draws all creatures back to their origin. Commenting on the relationship between divine and earthly love, S.H. Nasr makes an insightful observation about the Sufi concept of love which is useful in understanding Gāmi:

> The process of realization in Islamic spirituality involves becoming aware of the ever-expanding circle of what one loves until that ever-widening circle reaches the shore of Divinity and one realizes the love of God and, moreover, becomes aware that this love is the only real love (*al-ishq al-haqiqi*), while all other love is metaphorical love (*al-ishq al-majazi*) and a reflection of that one real love that, in the words of Dante at the end of his *Divine Comedy*, 'moves the sun and the stars'.[37]

Gāmi's poem 'Põmpir Nāmah' (The Moth's Tale) exploits the well-known image of a moth sacrificing itself on the candle's flame.[38] Here the idea of love as self-sacrifice that guarantees immortality takes the form of a delightful dialogue between the moth—a symbol of utmost devotion and sacrifice—and other insects, the on-lookers who are bewildered by the self-immolating passion of the moth. Only those who are ready to sacrifice themselves for the sake of love earn immortality.

> The flies searched for a candle frantically
> and found one burning alone.
> They pledged their love

and fluttered around its flame.
But flinched from flinging themselves into
its devouring fire.

Alas for those who set out in earnest
but leave the journey half-way!
Such stragglers only bring
shame to the lovers.

And then the moth rushed to the flame
and burnt himself up,
without a sob, a cry or a complaint.
He did the lovers proud.

Alas, no one has the courage of the moth!
And no one nears what he conquers with ease

Mahmud, dying for the Friend is the highest bliss
One who dies for love dies the death of a martyr

In yet another powerful poem 'Tamsīl-e Ādam' (The Parable of Man), Gāmi weaves a beautiful tapestry of interconnected images held together by a central image—that of an air bubble in the water. The poem starts with a question that runs through it as a refrain in the original: how is it that the bubble survives in the midst of water? The bubble, the poem suggests, has no existence apart from the water that surrounds it. The likeness of man to the bubble lies in this: just like the bubble originates in the water and is constantly sustained by it, man, too, originates in God and lives his every moment only through an unremitting sustenance from Him. Thus, like the bubble that has no existence outside the water, man has no existence outside of God or the 'great ocean of being' as mystics sometimes put it.

> I inquired of the bubble
> the parable of man
> 'Reveller, how do you stay alive in water?'

> 'Clutch at the rope of contemplation,
> Pull at the pulley of remembrance.
> Your soul's wheel will whirl in a dance
> like it's pulled with a rope.
> Let not joys and dreams waylay you'.

> Out of love
> the Lover blew,
> the bubble was born.
> He blew again,
> it mingled with water.
> What has perished?
> What left for reckoning?

The poem also uses other images like the burning kebab, waterwheel, pulley, boat, rose, fragrance, among others, to suggest how the soul should undertake its journey towards self-realization. The idea of God's immanence, evoked through the Prophet's proximity to Him, on the one hand, and to his companions, on the other, seems to be pivotal to the poem. The soul's proper journey, as Ibn Arabi explains, is not from a state of separation from God to union with Him but in realizing that it is already one with Him. This state of oneness, however, does not imply a complete identification of man and God. Just like the bubble—though it arises from water and mingles with it again—cannot be identified with the water that gives birth to it. A saying attributed to Ibn Arabi: 'A servant is a servant how much he might ascend/and God is God how much He might descend' (*al-abdu abdun in taraqqa/wa al-rabbu rabbun in tanazzala*), captures the subtle point. Gāmi's mysticism can be termed as theistic mysticism which posits the soul's proximity to, and not absorption into, God as its highest achievement, the latter being a characteristic feature of monistic mysticism or idealistic pantheism. It would, therefore, be a mistake to regard Gāmi as an upholder of the latter.

Like much other Sufi poetry, Gāmi uses the symbol of wine for divine intoxication and the wineserver for the divine beloved. Another poem, 'Kalewāl' (The Wine Server) begins as follows:

> Would that I could lay down my head
> for that wine server
> that thief of wits
> who beguiled me with a single trick
> and made me drunk
> on a heady wine!

His earthen cup
more fragrant than the perfume
infuses sweetness into me.
He pours the wine of gnosis
into the cup
And I drink it up.

~

Death is one of the major thematic concerns in Gāmi's verse. While in some poems, death is presented as an emancipating force delivering the humans from the sorrows of life, in some others an awareness of the brevity of life intensifies the need to love and be loved. In *masnavis* like 'Layla Majnun' and 'Yusuf Zulaykha', the lovers' continuity in the afterlife is clearly implied. However, in some lyrics the inevitability of death creates an urgency to seize the day before life slips away. The speaker in these lyrics reminds the beloved of the ravages bound to wreck the physical beauty and the final disintegration before death.

We have not come here to stay
The earth will devour us soon
And once dead, we will turn to dust
This longing will not wane!

My seething passion brooks no silence
And the pain dwindles not a bit
Come and play your lute and rebeck
My longing heart knows no peace![39]

Gāmi is a life-affirming poet celebrating beauty, pleasure and joy in existence. And yet, he is acutely aware of life's tragic fragility. Hence, a mood of sadness permeates many of his poems:

The world is but an abode of grief
Fathom this truth, my dear self!

Many a lively youth came here
Only to leave full of remorse
Like a rose they wilted on the bower
Fathom this truth, my dear self![40]

~

To whom shall I speak
of the sorrow within?
O my self, a poor wayfarer!
In the world's market I decked a shop
Alas, my trade fetched me no gains
Soon I will leave empty-handed
O my self, a poor wayfarer![41]

Many of the poems combine verses celebrating love's joys and those dealing with its trials, its fears and losses, and other vicissitudes attendant upon it:

How can I be merry when
the pain of love frets my heart?
I can only weep.
Love's raging fire melts my marrow

Its morbid fever scorches my liver
I languish in despair
Give me a cure.[42]

Since Islamic eschatology presents death as a momentous event—the gateway to either eternal bliss or damnation—Gāmi treats it with passionate intensity:

Your diminishing strength is a sign of death
Your greying hair is a signal too
Your heart is stony still, what a shame!
Know that the world is a vale of tears

Illness and pain are but ploys of death
Look, where they all lead to
Speechless are all humans before it

When the angel of death will show up
You will not escape his stinging breath
All noise and levity will turn to air[43]

Literary Genres

Vatsun

A great portion of Kashmiri poetry available today has been transmitted orally from one generation to the next. Owing to the fact that the Kashmiri poetic tradition remained predominantly an oral one, it is not surprising that sometimes numerous variations of a single poem attributed to a poet are found in various manuscripts. How a particular poem was remembered and passed on therefore determined how it was finally written. Oral declamation of poetry hence continued to have immense importance even into the 20th century. Kashmiri poets seem to have been conscious of the oral-aural mode of their poems and exploited their performative quality quite successfully. Lyric poetry thus lived in the memories of the masses, finding a secure place there because every native speaker would emotionally respond to it, although not many had the competence to understand the complex ideas that were sometimes treated in it.

The *vatsun*, unique to Kashmiri, has been its pre-eminent literary form through centuries. Structurally, the *vatsun* is divided into a number of stanzas ending with a refrain called *vōj*. Different from both Lalla Ded's mystical *vākh* and Sheikh Nuruddin's didactic *shruk*, the *vatsun* is primarily a love lyric, although mystical, devotional and homiletic *vatsuns* also abound in Kashmiri. Habba Khatoon (1554–1609) is the first poet of love *vatsuns* which have gained immense popularity. J.L. Kaul's description of the Kashmiri love lyric, despite its limitations, is nonetheless useful:

The chief contribution of this period is, however, a new kind of song which tells of secular human love. This is the *lōl* lyric, a song set to music, wherein the poet sings of his *lōl*, a Kashmiri word signifying an untranslatable complex of love, longing and a tugging at the heart. The *lōl* lyric is a short poem, an utterance of a single mood, rarely in more than six or ten lines, including the refrain. It is a thing of music, a very melodious music, with its end-rhymes and medial rhymes and ever-recurring refrains, its alliterations and assonances that come naturally as the very stuff of the language which has a high proportion of vowels and semi-vowels to its consonants, and in which aspirates, gutterals [sic] and harsh consonants are rare. There is a looseness and a flexibility of rhythm as in the verse of Lal Dyad, and the metre is not yet made to fit in quite within the precision of Persian quantitative pattern. It is not an intellectual lyric, it states no theme.[44]

It is believed that the *vatsun* had its origin in folk songs whose indelible mark it bears. A widespread opinion, endorsed by J.L. Kaul in the quote above, also suggests that the language of *vatsun* is not sophisticated and relies mainly on music for its effect. Spontaneity and an elemental simplicity of thought and feeling are thought to be its defining features. Due to its affinity with the folk song, the *vatsun* is also seen as lacking intellectual depth. Characterized by both internal and end rhymes, rhythm, alliteration and assonance, the *vatsun*, in this opinion, is little more than 'a thing of music'.

Apart from the fact that the above description of the *vatsun* is too general, it is also flawed, at least partly. As a genre, the *vatsun* has exhibited remarkable adaptability and embraced themes and motifs of various types. Although the repetition of the refrain (*võj*) in the *vatsun* obstructs its smooth flow, and alliteration, assonance and rhyme impart to it a musical quality, it would be wrong to define it as a poem that characteristically lacks verbal subtlety and intellectual depth or shows little development of thought. Unlike a folk song, the *vatsun* exhibits all those qualities which make it fit for the expression of a broad range of ideas and feelings. Again, unlike a folk song, the *vatsun* is not the ritualistic expression of community values. As we shall see, Gāmi's *vatsuns* cover a broad range of themes and engage the reader's imagination at a deep level. In Gāmi, the *vatsun* also acquires a new complexity becoming, in the words of Jonathan Culler, 'a repertoire of discursive possibilities: complaint, praise, hope, and suffering, relating inner and outer worlds'.[45]

Writing about Gāmi's significant intervention in Kashmir's literary history, Naji Munawar and Shafi Shauq remark, 'The river of Kashmiri poetry came to a halt in the Afghan period once more and except Mahmud Gāmi all other Kashmiri poets seem to have fallen dumb'.[46] They further point out that the poets who wrote in Kashmiri such as Fakhir, Sādullah Shah Ābādi, Baba Kamāl, Mir Abdullah and Mulla Ubaidullah were primarily poets of the Persian language and a single feature that characterizes their poetry was a departure from the traditional *vatsun* in favour of more purely Persian forms. Gāmi, therefore, assumes importance for Munawar and Shauq because he made the *vatsun*—an indigenous poetic form—truly versatile.

Kashmiri literary criticism has so far not developed a theory of the *vatsun* to address some of the problems peculiar to it. In Western literary criticism, the lyric was not given adequate attention for a long time probably because Aristotle in his seminal work *Poetics* had paid scant attention to it, focussing exclusively on mimetic genres. The Romantic revolution established the primacy of the lyric—which was for a long time read as an expression of intense and individual experience. This tendency witnessed a reversal of sorts when the Anglo-American New Criticism emerged as the most influential school of literary criticism in the 1930s. With their insistence that all lyrical poetry is, at bottom, a kind of drama, it was not difficult to see how a sharp distinction was assumed between the poet and the speaker in the poem.[47]

Jonathan Culler, in his recent work *Theory of the Lyric* (2015), offers an insightful study of the lyric suggesting that it be read as a kind of performance of an event rather than the description and interpretation of a past event:

> The fundamental characteristic of lyric, I am arguing, is not the description and interpretation of a past event but the iterative and iterable performance of an event in the lyric present, in the special 'now', of lyric articulation.[48]

In Kashmiri literary criticism, scant attention has been paid to distinguishing between poets as historical figures and their literary personae, and the lyric has been read largely as an autobiographical expression of a real life. The Romantic model which reads it as an unmediated representation of the poet's consciousness is assumed to be true. A case in point is that of Habba Khatoon, whose poetry is almost invariably read as personal confession. It seems very probable that the anecdotes about her personal life took shape only after her lyrics were read like that. This approach quite often leads to specious biographical speculation about the author. As Victor Erlich writes:

> What may seem on the surface to be a reflection of psychic reality may at closer range turn out to be an aesthetic formula superimposed on this reality; . . . whatever experience—communal or personal— finds expression in poetry is always formed or deformed in line with the exigencies of the given poetic genre.[49]

It is important, therefore, from a critical point of view, not to conflate the 'poetic I', which may assume different forms within the poetic world, with the 'empirical I' of the poet. As Paul Losensky has argued convincingly while discussing the genre of the *ghazal*, 'The "I" that speaks in the poem is as much a product of precedent and tradition as of the poet's own experience.'[50]

It should be noted, however, that if it is fallacious to read the *vatsun* exclusively as an expression of the poet's subjective experience, it is equally questionable to regard it only as a fictional imitation of a persona, as a mere literary posturing. It is true that the Kashmiri love lyric (*lōl vatsun*) typically depicts a lovesick woman either addressing her unresponsive male lover or a friend to whom she unburdens her heart, yet not all *vatsuns* can be read as dramatic monologues asking the reader to reconstruct the context of the speaker.

Generally speaking, it is difficult for the reader to say which poems embody the genuine expression of an idea or feeling the poets have themselves experienced. However, Gāmi's lyrics, like those of many other Kashmiri poets, do provide a clue for identifying the speaking voice. A typical love *vatsun* will have a dramatic context, usually a lovesick female speaker, but such a context will be missing in a mystical or religious *vatsun* where the poet seems to be directly addressing the reader. The reader can, therefore, make out whether it is a character or personae responding to a situation or an expression of the poet's consciousness.

Moreover, within a single lyric there sometimes occur frequent shifts of address; a poem, for example, may begin with the typical lovelorn speaker addressing an absent lover and yet be interspersed with lines directly addressed by the poet to the reader. Or there can be a shift from the female speaker to the male and vice versa within a single poem. Contrary to what critics like Trilokinath Raina have asserted, the

Kashmiri *vatsun* is not characterized by a single mood or tone throughout.[51] The signature verse—in which the poet speaks directly in his/her name before signing off—further illustrates this idea of the shift. Gāmi's corpus abounds in lyrics which reveal a combination of the direct and dramatic modes.

Failing to appreciate this shift and assuming that the speaker in a *vatsun* is consistently a single voice, Āzād picks a few poems by Gāmi, Maqbool Shah Krālwāri, Rasul Mir and Azizullah Haqāni, as instances of the beloved suddenly, and unwarrantedly, changing from male to female. He cites a *vatsun* of Gāmi beginning with 'My summer jasmine has turned pallid' (*aerini rang gõm shrāvne hiye*), wondering how a poem which has a female speaker-lover throughout suddenly springs a surprise on the reader with 'She showed me a glimpse beneath the veil' (*ruakh hõvnam burqe tale*), suggesting that the beloved is now a female. As discussed above, a proper criticism of the *vatsun* requires a more nuanced approach than this, to account for its rich variety and complexity.

Gāmi is also credited with introducing another lyric form, the *ghazal*, into Kashmiri. Though resembling *vatsun* closely, the *ghazal* is still distinct from it.[52] Unlike the narrative form (*masnavi*) where Gāmi exhibited a rare skill in adapting the Persian models, the *ghazal* does not seem to have been his forte. Apart from very few poems which can be characterized as *ghazal*, his lyrics fall in the category of the *vatsun*. It was his younger contemporary Rasul Mir who emerged as the first mature voice in the Kashmiri ghazal, although a strict separation between the two forms is still difficult in him, and it was not before the 20th century that the *ghazal* reached its zenith.[53]

Although the *vatsun* has ceased to have the same resonance in the 21st century that it enjoyed a century or so ago, it has left a deep impression on the *ghazal*, a form preferred by most poets today. The *vatsun*, however, clearly parts company with the Persian *ghazal* in one thing: the homoerotic aspect of the latter is entirely missing in the former. Also, the lack of gender-specific pronouns in Persian stands in a marked contrast to Kashmiri. While in case of Persian, this lack results in a kind of ambivalence regarding the beloved's gender, in Kashmiri the gender of neither the speaker nor the beloved can remain ambiguous.

Masnavi

The *masnavi* can be defined as a narrative poem in rhyming couplets. It was the first Persian genre adapted into Kashmiri. Gāmi is aware of his rare gift of telling tales. In 'Yusuf Zulaykha', he writes:

> Listen to poor Mahmud's wails
> His wonderful gift of telling tales

Gāmi wrote ten *masnavis*, almost all of them adaptations from the Persian models of Nizāmi, Attār, Rumi and Jāmi. According to some critics, 'Khusrau

Shīrīn', written by Gāmi in 1781 when he was twenty-six, is the first *masnavi* in Kashmiri.[54] The poem, a romantic narrative, is adapted from Nizāmi and is set in the court of Sasanians, the last pre-Islamic dynasty to rule the Persian world. It recounts the love of King Khusrau Parvaiz and an Armenian princess Shīrīn. The story is full of unexpected turns and reversals and in Gāmi's adaption gains a pace that is missing in Nizāmi. Gāmi omits many details of Nizāmi and wraps up the romance in about 700-odd couplets.

While Nizāmi's poem moves at a leisurely pace, Gāmi's is fast-paced. In Nizāmi's *masnavi*, Shīrīn urges Khusrau to wrest his kingdom from Bahram Chubin. Annoyed at this demand, Khusrau leaves Shīrīn and travels to Byzantium where Heraclius, its emperor, gives him his daughter Maryam in marriage and helps him defeat Bahram Chubin in a battle. Gāmi omits all these details, in addition to the numerous stories that Shīrīn's maidens tell Khusrau when he asks them to do so. As if aware of Hellmut Ritter, the German Orientalist who said that one could eliminate a third of Nizāmi's poem without obscuring the action, Gāmi reduces Nizāmi's narrative to less than one-third.[55] Despite this brevity, Gāmi achieves his aim of presenting in Kashmiri all the important strands of the story.

While Khusrau falls instantly in love with Shīrīn when his confidante Shāpur describes her to him vividly in one of the most graphic passages written by Gāmi, she is smitten with him when Shāpur, disguised as a hermit, enters her garden and hangs Khusrau's portrait on a tree. From the moment her eyes fall upon the portrait, Shīrīn is struck by its spectacular beauty and is filled with an intense desire to meet Khusrau. The entry of Farhād, a skilled stonecutter who falls in love with Shīrīn at first sight but conceals his love because he is aware of Shīrīn's devotion to Khusrau, throws into relief the contrasting figures of the two rivals for the love of Shīrīn. Farhād, however, is fated never to achieve his goal.

Khusrau, alarmed by Farhād's success in digging a canal through Mount Bīsutun, eliminates him with a cunning ploy. The middle section of the *masnavi* also revolves around Khusrau's frustrated passion for Shīrīn as she repels his advances and refuses to surrender to him outside of marriage. Indignant at Shīrīn's attitude, Khusrau seeks other women but soon tires of them and longs for his first love. The narrative is marked by separations and joyful reunions but ends tragically as Khusrau becomes a victim of patricide and Shīrīn kills herself to escape from the lust of Khusrau's son by Maryam, Shiruya.

'Khusrau Shīrīn' is set in pre-Islamic Persia and is the only *masnavi* of Gāmi which deals with mundane or earthly love with no mystical overtones. This, however, is not to suggest that the poem lacks an ethical dimension because, among other things, it offers a contrast between Khusrau's self-indulgence and opportunism and Farhād's utter devotion to Shīrīn. The verbal duel between Khusrau and Farhād in which the latter clearly trumps the former, marks, in the words of Hashmat Moayyad,

> the culmination of the clash between two conflicting codes and concepts of love, one heroic and sensual, regarding the beloved as a prize or booty to be conquered and possessed, the other unrequited and all-consuming, relishing the very notion of the annihilation of the self through love.[56]

Khusrau is depicted as a king whose actions are motivated by self-interest and who seeks dominion in love, too, making use of his position to remove Farhād from his path and treating Shīrīn rather whimsically. Farhād, on the other hand, is a suffering lover whose death symbolizes the idea of self-sacrifice. Shīrīn, despite Khusrau's ill treatment, is devoted to him but exhibits extreme self-respect in not surrendering to him on his terms. Khusrau's treachery which sends Farhād to his death recoils on him as he becomes a victim of the treachery of his own son. It was not for nothing that Nizāmi calls his poem *havas nāmah,* 'a story of passion'.

Throughout the romance, Gāmi combines elaborate hyperbole with straightforward narration of events. The episodes of Khusrau's passion for Shīrīn, her guarded requital of this passion, Farhād's love for Shīrīn and Khusrau's scheming against Farhād, and many more strands, are woven into a whole. Despite this selective adaptation, Gāmi manages a continuous and unbroken narrative movement in the poem.

~

Adapted from Jāmi's famous romance, 'Yusuf Zulaykha' is perhaps the best-known *masnavi* of Gāmi. Translated into Latin by the German Orientalist Karl Bukhardt in 1895, the *masnavi* has enjoyed a wide circulation in Kashmir and was one of the primary reasons for its popularity. Naji Munawar and Shafi Shauq call 'Yusuf Zulaykha' the most popular Kashmiri *masnavi* ever written, beating even Maqbool Shah Kralwari's celebrated *masnavi* 'Gulrez' in popularity.[57]

Betrayal, envy, jealousy, reunion, forgiveness, patience, filial impiety, all feature in 'Yusuf Zulaykha'. The story based on the Quranic Chapter XII 'Yusuf' has inspired countless poems in numerous languages centred on both romantic and mystical love. It has been read both as a love story as well as a moral tale. The Quranic narrative is about Yusuf's journey from Canaan where as a child he becomes the victim of his half-brothers' fierce jealousy, is thrown by them into a well, is salvaged by a passing caravan and sold as a slave in Egypt.

Bought by a nobleman in Egypt, he soon becomes an object of passionate desire of his wife, described by the Quran simply as 'the nobleman's wife'. Yusuf resists her temptations but, having repulsed her advances, falls a victim to her hurt pride and lands in the prison where he stays for several years. Gifted with a rare ability to interpret dreams correctly, he is not only released from the prison but also raised to the position of a minister in Egypt. The Quranic narrative foregrounds Yusuf's piety, patience and forgiveness, especially his exemplary conduct in resisting the temptations of 'the nobleman's wife'. The narrative which the Quran calls *ahsanul qasas*, 'the best of stories', owing to its unmistakable moral lesson becomes a love story in the hands of poets like Jāmi.[58]

Although some adaptations of the story show a narrative tension between a condemnation of Zulaykha for using guile to seduce Yusuf and an admiration for her complete devotion and love for him, Gāmi—following Jāmi—projects her love as a manifestation of divine love and nowhere suggests an indictment of her acts. The story, therefore, becomes less of a moral tale than an allegory for the nature of true love. Rather than presenting Zulaykha as a dangerous scheming seductress, Gāmi's poem inscribes her in his paradigm of the eternal relationship between beauty (*jamāl* or *husn*) and love (*ishq*). Zulaykha becomes a symbol of love's eternal yearning for beauty symbolized by Yusuf. When the two finally meet, Yusuf restores her to her earlier state of beauty and receives divine sanction to marry her. The love that Yusuf feels for her suggests that Zulaykha is rewarded for her unswerving devotion and fidelity to Yusuf. Her death out of grief for Yusuf marks the culmination of the idea of love as total self-sacrifice.

The story symbolizes the triumph of true love over all odds. Zulaykha's passion for Yusuf transforms into an awakening which leads her to renounce her false creed and embrace that of Yusuf. Her love for Yusuf does not diminish but achieves a kind of sublimation bringing about her transformation. It is notable that in Gāmi's *masnavi*, Yusuf's character is eclipsed by Zulaykha's. While Gāmi expends a lot of effort in describing Yusuf's beauty and his charismatic effect on others, it is Zulaykha who emerges as the most remarkable figure in the poem. From the moment, in the beginning of the poem, when she sees Yusuf repeatedly in her dreams to the last moment when she falls dead on Yusuf's tomb, Zulaykha is by far Gāmi's most powerful and memorable character. The poem also contains some of the most beautiful songs in Kashmiri sung by Zulaykha.

~

'Layla Majnun' is a very popular narrative romance adapted from Nizāmi, which he wrote in 1188. The story is Arabic in origin and was based on a collection of love poems originating in the 8th century and attributed to Qais who later became known as Majnun-e Layla (Layla's Majnun) in Arabic folklore. No other poem in world literature has seen as many imitations and translations as 'Layla Majnun'.[59] Gāmi was the first to adapt it into Kashmiri.

There are a number of significant departures from Nizāmi's poem. Gāmi omits many episodes from Nizāmi's original: it has neither a prologue nor an epilogue and hence lacks a certain framework within which Nizāmi holds his narrative. Gāmi also omits episodes like Majnun's pilgrimage to Mecca after he is rejected by Layla's father, Ibn Salām's asking Layla's father for her hand, Majnun's meeting with Prince Nawfal who promises to marry him to Layla, the battle between Nawfal and Layla's tribe, Salām of Baghdad's meeting with Majnun, Layla's marriage to Ibn Salām and his death, and Zayd's dreams of the lovers' ultimate union in Paradise.

A significant departure from Nizāmi is the episode in which Majnun, having finally made it to Layla's place as bridegroom and waiting for his much-cherished prize, throws it all away by an outrageous act. As Layla's puppy strays into the august gathering of nobles, Majnun picks it up and starts kissing and caressing it. Shocked by this, Layla's kinsmen drive away Majnun and all the guests from the assembly. Thereafter, Majnun returns to the wilderness to spend the rest of his days in sorrow and longing. Among the Persian adaptations of Nizāmi's poem, those by Jāmi and Amir Khusrau are quite well known but neither contains the puppy episode although both mention Majnun's encounter with 'Layla's dog', that is, a dog from Layla's street and hence dear to Majnun. In Gāmi's version, Majnun's reply to Layla's complaint underscores the mystical interpretation of the story:

'O crazy lover, see what you have done?
Why grumble now, you threw away your chance?

Had you shown a little more caution
Our love would have attained fruition

Why did you lose your mind there?
And leave the assembly in frenzy?'

'Listen, O beauty, to what I say
Love's fire had burnt down my soul

Reason is Love's handmaiden
Love leads to the secrets hidden

Reason is sluggish, Love swift of action
Love is like the king, Reason his vizier

Knowing nothing of Love, Jibrīl wonders
How it found a way to God's presence!

Your love has made me quit reason and sense
This is why I am slighted by the men of Reason

If I possessed reason and smartness
I would know the cure for my suffering

The frenzied ones dispense with discernment
They cherish vision more than union'

In addition to inscribing Majnun in the class of *malāmāti* lovers, those who purposely abase themselves before others to show their pure devotion in love, the episode also serves as an artistic device through which the imminent union of the lovers is averted. In all versions and adaptations of the romance there is no physical intimacy of the lovers and both die without consummating their love. So, although the lovers have suffered immensely for the union, when the moment for it comes, it is transcended entirely, the consummation of love being inadmissible in the design of the story.[60]

The image of the legendary Majnun with its origins in Udhrite Arabic poetry persists in all the subsequent adaptations of the romance including Gāmi's. Pathos, madness, self-denial and extreme devotion in love characterize Majnun.[61] The plot in Gāmi becomes even more slender due to the omissions stated above, throwing into a sharper relief Majnun's pathetic state. Love in 'Layla Majnun' is depicted as an overwhelming and possessive force that reduces the protagonist Majnun to a helpless state. By the moral standards of his time, Majnun is guilty of filial impiety. When his parents plead importunely before him to return home and give up frenzy, he excuses himself, declaring that love is an irresistible force. Gāmi skilfully intertwines the twin strands of eroticism and asceticism within a single narrative. The story of 'Layla Majnun' has been traditionally read both as a great poem of earthly love and a mystical allegory. Gāmi, however, foregrounds the mystical dimension of the poem as the passage quoted above demonstrates. Despite its merits, 'Layla Majnun' is not on a par with some other *masnavis* of Gāmi especially 'Yusuf Zulaykha', 'Khusrau and Shīrīn' and 'Sheikh San'ān'.

~

'Sheikh San'ān' is a narrative poem adapted from a story in Attār's "Mantiqut Tayr"' about a Muslim savant who becomes miserable after falling in love with an infidel girl. In Attār's story the girl is Christian and a resident of Rome. Gāmi replaces the Christian with a Hindu girl and uses local markers to give a native touch to the poem. Curiously though, the setting is still Rome, the heartland of Christendom. A remarkable thing about the poem is the inclusion of a song in it where San'ān gives vent to his deep love for the unnamed Hindu girl. Quite in keeping with Gāmi's practice in other *masnavis*, the song here breaks the flow of the otherwise quick-paced narrative.

At your bidding Sheikh San'ān renounced his piety
O Hindu girl, my bewitching love, give ear to my wails!

The world is a mirage, how many have wasted away!
Heal my pain, be pleased with me, my love is very deep

Don't put on airs, all lives will end on a shriek of
mourning
O Hindu girl, my bewitching love, give ear to my
wails!

The girl, conceited and dismissive of San'ān to begin
with, gives in before the beseeching lover on the
condition that he forsake his faith, burn his scripture
and become her swineherd, all extremely abominable
acts in the eyes of a Muslim. The woebegone Sheikh
agrees. He abjures his religion and devotes himself
wholeheartedly to her. Shocked by this, his disciples
return with a heavy heart to Mecca but continue to
pray for their master's redemption. Finally, their
prayers are answered. Sheikh San'ān is reclaimed
but only after love has transformed him entirely. His
transformation lies in awakening to the importance of
sacrifice and true meaning of love—without sacrificing
one's dearest things there can be no real worship. In
loving an infidel girl Sheikh San'ān sacrificed his very
high reputation and honour as a great sage and leader
of the believers. Love, Gāmi suggests, demands such
sacrifice.

What is remarkable is that love's transformative
power encompasses the infidel girl, too, as her
brusqueness disappears under its influence. She,
despite herself, falls deeply in love with the Sheikh
and, through a sudden epiphany, realizes the truth of
his creed. She accepts San'ān's faith and realizes the
futility of the world and its glamour. Falling to his feet,

she begs him for mercy and requital of love. But now the Sheikh has passed beyond the allurements of the physical realm. He admonishes her to give up self-love and embrace the love of God. In a moving passage towards the end of the poem, the girl breathes her last, having experienced an identical spiritual awakening as that of the Sheikh.

'O Hindu girl, what do you desire?
The love you ask for is alien to me

What for are your blandishments?
Your beguilement is in vain

Why do you deck your locks?
Appearance no longer lures me

Don't exult in glamour and riches
Don't flaunt your mole and tresses

Lay off pride and envy
Cleanse your heart of rust

Abjure your ego and self-love
You will realize your essence'

'My selfhood has vanished
Command me and I will obey'

He gave her some crucial lessons
She proclaimed the *kalimah*

'Strive for that which is worthy
Adam's form is a mere sketch

Form flickers and peters out
Form is a slave to the essence

Think not of life as a trifle
Cleanse yourself of all dross

Get over selfhood's obstacle
Your love abides within you

Your ego is an impediment
Don't stumble, get over it'

Twice she uttered God's holy name
And surrendered her soul to Him

Remember this each day
Dying so is a blessing

She attained union fast
And died a saint's death

Mahmud Gāmi has no more to say
This was Sheikh San'ān's tale

The poem illustrates the idea of the transformation of profane into divine love. This motif of the transmutation of metaphorical love (*ishq-i majāzi*) into real love (*ishq-i haqīqi*) was valued highly by some Sufis.[62] Love, the poem suggests, is more than an attraction between the opposite sexes. Earthly love leads to suffering, and suffering cleanses the heart of all impurities—self-love and the love of the world—and prepares one to receive the gift of divine love. The ordeal that Sheikh San'ān experiences makes him realize the true meaning of love and leads him from the love of appearance and form to the love of the essence. The physical charms of the girl trap him but the suffering that ensues chastises him.

That the Sufi poets like Attār thought it necessary to adhere to what they believed was the right religious creed is borne out by the Christian girl's act of conversion to Islam. Gāmi follows Attār here and has the Hindu girl convert to Islam to realize the highest spiritual goal. In Attār's narrative, however, the Christian girl has a dream in which she is directed to seek out San'ān and follow his religious path. Gāmi, instead, shows the Hindu girl melt before San'ān's desperate pleading. He also opts for a shorter meter and leaves out some details from Attār's story, making the narrative swifter and crisper than Attār's.

~

Another narrative poem by Gāmi 'Mansur Nāmah' (Mansur's Tale) recounts the story of the famous mystic Husayn bin Mansur Al-Hallāj (d. 922). Hallāj is a very controversial figure in the history of Islam and has evoked both admiration and severe censure till this day. Known for his declaration *anal haq*, 'I am the Truth', the most notorious utterance in the history of Sufism, Mansur's contested legacy continues to draw attention today. Although severely criticized by early historians like Tabari and Nadīm, the author of *Fihrist*, it was not long before the Sufi poets revisited his *anal haq* from a new perspective and inscribed him as a martyr for love in their poetry.

Louis Massignon (1883–1962), a French scholar, spent a substantial portion of his life researching Mansur's life and thought, and produced a magnum opus *The Passion of Hallaj* (1922), a work of formidable scholarship in four volumes. According to sources, Mansur was crucified for the charges of blasphemy, his utterance *anal haq* being interpreted as a direct challenge to the Islamic creed of God's transcendence and absolute unity. The years following his execution witnessed a reversal in the public perception of Mansur. Sufi chroniclers like Ali Hujwiri (d. 1072) in his famous *Kashful Mahjub* started the work of rehabilitating Mansur.

Attār eulogized him and interpreted his seemingly blasphemous utterance by comparing it with the utterance that came from the burning bush which addressed Moosa (the Biblical Moses) as 'I am your Lord', thus following Mansur who in his collection of sermons titled *Tawāsīn* had compared himself to

Moosa's burning bush. Rumi in his *Masnavi* compared Mansur to the red-hot iron in the midst of a fire which imagines itself to be the fire while in his prose work *Fihi ma fihi* he interpreted it as a supreme expression of selflessness. Having forgotten himself entirely in God, Mansur lost all sense of selfhood. His 'I' was therefore in total contrast to Pharoah's only apparently similar assertion of 'I', which was in fact a declaration of apotheosis (*bud anal haq dar lab-e Mansur nur/ bud anallah dar lab-e Firawn zur*). Gradually the opinion that the custodians of religious law had misunderstood *anal haq* became quite common.

Mansur, it was said, through claiming that he was the Truth was neither claiming divinity or incarnation, nor denying God's transcendence but pointing to an equally important aspect of the divine: a profound truth of God's immanence in His creation. Mansur was thus immortalized by poets as the leader of enraptured gnostics who capture a truth which evades most people. His fault, according to the famous Persian poet Hafiz, was that he divulged a great secret before the commoners.[63] S.H. Nasr makes the following observation about Mansur, 'His *anal haqq* (I am the Truth) has become perennial witness to the fact that Sufism is essentially gnosis and that ultimately it is God within us who utters "I" once the veil of otherness has been removed.'[64]

Having instigated the keepers of the law with his recklessness, Mansur was arrested and tried for the grave charge of blasphemy. Claiming divinity and preaching incarnationism were offences punishable with death. Mansur was lashed, his limbs cut off and was hanged on the gibbet in 922 in Baghdad. Curiously, Gāmi puts the words *bu chus khoda* 'I am God' in Mansur's mouth instead of *anal haq* thus stripping the original of its inherent equivocality. The narrative proceeds without much dramatic force, nor is there any attempt to bring alive the character of Mansur. The focus throughout seems to be on the contrast between those who can only see the apparent and those who can penetrate the veil of appearance. Mansur's each fibre proclaims 'I am God/the Truth' even after his body is cut to pieces and reduced to ashes.

~

In yet another shorter *masnavi* 'Paheal Nāmah' (The Shepherd's Tale)—adapted from Rumi's *masnavi*—Moosa overhears a shepherd singing away, addressing God in grossly concrete and crude terms, thus betraying a damnable ignorance of proper etiquette. Moosa sharply reprimands the rustic shepherd and reminds him of God's incomparability and freedom from all wants. God, however, has loved the shepherd's prayer and commands Moosa to find him and tell him to keep saying the same prayer. Moosa learns the lesson: what counts with God is sincerity of the heart and not the refinement of manners.

Moosa humbled himself, saying: 'My dear one
Your anguished heart is dear to your Lord.

Your heart's bane has turned into boon
Your blasphemy has fetched a very high price.

So, keep saying what you said before
The good God says he is pleased with you.

Care not for manners and protocols
Say fearlessly what your heart holds'.

Long live O love, our sweet frenzy!
O the cure of all our ills!

O the cure of our pride and self-love
O you our Plato and Galen!

The mould of dust rises to heaven through love
The mountains start dancing and gain vision.

Love infused life into the Mount Sinai
Sinai got drunk and Moosa fell unconscious.

~

Gāmi's adaptation of Persian *masnavis* raises some
interesting points. None of the *masnavis* is translated
or adapted in full. Gāmi leaves out the long prefaces
which provide a framework to the Persian *masnavis*.

Commenting on the function that literary adaptation can perform, Miriam Edlich-Muth has observed:

> . . . adaptation can be seen as a process by which every retelling of a tale shines a new light on the multiplicitous narrative potential of a given story, thereby necessarily re-casting the narrative as a whole . . . it is when details of a narrative have been changed or recontextualized in order to contribute to a new understanding that they can offer the most interesting insights into how the source text was being re-shaped by its interaction with a different linguistic or regional community.[65]

We witness a range of practices in Gāmi's translation–adaptation—omissions, additions, digressions, condensation—all of which strengthen the idea of translation as a re-creation in a new context than a mere reproduction of the original.

A look at 'Layla Majnun' will shed light on Gāmi's translation–adaptation practice. Not only does Gāmi omit many episodes of Nizāmi's poem, he also adds a few such as Majnun disguising himself as a blind beggar to visit Layla, his meeting a shepherd and putting on a ram's skin to mix with Layla's flock to have her glimpse, his entering into a garden and saving a fir tree from the axe of a woodcutter, and the appearance of a rival (raqīb) who wants to kill Majnun but is paralysed mysteriously first and then cured by the prayer of Majnun. This suggests that Gāmi knew some other adaptations of the romance, for example, by Abdullah Hātifi (d. 1520) which includes some of these episodes and chose to draw upon both the versions of Nizāmi and Hātifi, although the latter is not mentioned anywhere by him.

Some of the episodes Gāmi includes seem to have had no precedent in any variant of the romance. A case in point is that of Layla who hardly reacts to her parents' curbs on her in other variants, but in Gāmi's poem wittily responds to her mother and feigns complete ignorance of the emotion of love when reprimanded by her. To take another example, the following passage in which Majnun's father pleads with him not to abandon his parents, has no precedent in Nizāmi or any other adaptation of the romance and represents a local variation:

> If you abandon us, we will follow you
> Offer you our lives, sacrifice our souls
>
> A childless man faces neglect while alive
> Despite riches he is counted worthless
>
> A childless man gropes blindly in the dark
> Despite all, he remains uncared for
>
> A childless man finds no helping hand
> As he grows old, he meets with repudiation

He is like a leftover fruit on the tree
Blown away when the wind turns fierce

No one lends him a sympathetic ear
Vainly he wishes for a helping hand

No one awakes him from his sleep
And no one lulls him to pleasant dreams

Eid and *Herath* bring no joy to him
Like a tramp he seeks shelter in mosques

No one attends to him in distress
Vainly he waits for someone to come

Gāmi also intersperses his narratives with a number of songs, some of them of striking quality, which impart a distinctly Kashmiri colour to them. In 'Layla Majnun', however, one feels there are too many songs in the narrative which impede its smooth flow.

Some of Gāmi's *masnavis*, most notably 'Yusuf Zulaykha', 'Layla Majnun', 'Khusrau Shīrīn' and 'Sheikh San'ān', are focused on exploring the internal state of the characters, and external events bring to light aspects of their person. Gāmi uses monologue, dialogue, description, narratorial interjections and even songs very effectively in them. The action in these *masnavis* serves to reveal the inner character of the protagonists. The inner experience of the agents taking part in action therefore assumes primary importance in them. However, in some *masnavis* like 'Paheal Nāmah' and 'Mansur Nāmah', it is the storyline rather than the characters that keeps the reader engaged.

Gāmi and the Modern Reader

As this introduction has tried to demonstrate, an acute awareness of the transcendental dimension of existence pervades Gāmi's verse even where he treats romantic and earthly love. He is not unique in possessing this profound spiritual consciousness as all pre-modern Kashmiri poetry bears this mark. A secular poet, according to the sensibility prevalent in the literary milieu of the age, would have been a near contradiction in terms because even such a poetic theme as erotic love was invariably anchored in a religious or at least spiritual paradigm and could never have been conceived in secular terms.[66] An unfortunate trend that has witnessed a sharp rise in recent decades, especially in the works of translation of some well-known Sufi poets such as Rumi, places Sufi poetry outside the framework of faith and sometimes even alleges an opposition between the two. The fact, however, is that Sufi poetry presupposes a worldview which is conceivable only within a religious paradigm.

Again, the modern reader, with her secular sensibility oriented to an essentially this-worldly attitude and inclined to explore the ideological ramifications of particular texts, might be somewhat uneasy with the preponderance of themes such as divine love, mortality

and salvation in pre-modern poetry. In the Kashmiri
literary tradition, it is only in the 20th century that
poets turned their attention to what are called the
social and political issues of their times.

Such a reader can only be advised to be sensitive
to the metaphysical rootedness of the poetry under
question, for its full appreciation. To allege that the pre-
modern Kashmiri poets lacked a political consciousness
is to commit the heresy of critical anachronism as all
poetic themes in the pre-modern world were almost
invariably derived from religious ideas. Moreover, an
overriding concern with ahistorical themes does not
imply a negation of time and history because time is
itself seen from the perspective of the timeless and
eternal. The apparent disregard of the immediate
socio-political context, therefore, turns out to be,
paradoxically, an engagement with it.[67]

Another feature of Kashmiri poetry, exemplified
amply in Gāmi's verse, that the modern reader might
find a little quaint is its imagery. Quite often the
arched eyebrows of the beloved are compared to the
bow, the eyelashes to arrows, the nose to the dagger,
the curled locks to snakes, the waist to a strand of
hair, the face to the moon or the sun, and so on and
so forth. Here again, Kashmiri poetry exhibits the
influence of Persian genres. It is useful to remember
that lyrical poetry generally, but more particularly
the *ghazal* and the forms influenced by it, evince a
highly conventional nature. Charles Baudelaire, the
celebrated French poet, has identified hyperbole and

apostrophe as not only the most agreeable but also most necessary to a lyric.[68] Kashmiri poetry makes an abundant use of both devices.

Gāmi's Craftsmanship

At several places, Gāmi alludes to his popularity as a poet and at one place, at least, makes a comment on the art of writing poetry:

> Nizāmi was favoured by God's blessings
> I, Mahmud Gāmi, too, partake in them.
> Think of composing verse as piercing a pearl
> Or rending your heart-soul from your body.[69]

The image of piercing a pearl suggests a delicate craft. In one of his poems, Nizāmi who, as we have seen, is mentioned many times by Gāmi as a model worth emulating, compares the art of poetry to the handmaid who prepares a bride on her wedding, pointing thereby to its basic function of making something more beautiful by means of words. Poetry, in this view, makes no attempt to sound 'natural' or disguise its artifice. Gāmi's poems, even those on Sufi themes, testify to his craftsmanship in exploiting the sound and sense of words.

To illustrate this, let us look at Gāmi's striking use of imagery in two passages, one from 'Khusrau Shīrīn' where Shāpur is describing Shīrīn's beauty to Khusrau and the other from 'Layla Majnun' which describes the beginning of love between Layla and Qais (Majnun). The passages reveal how even conventional and worn images can be used by a master craftsman to create fresh meanings. They also demonstrate the striking manner of linking a thought to image.

I

If perchance gazelles catch a glimpse of her
The kohl-rimmed eyes leave them stunned

Since those eyes have bewitched the gazelles
They have hidden themselves in the forests

Those eyes have made the narcissus sick
Its head has dropped down in shame

Those eyes are like two springs of wine
Her coquettishness too thrills like wine

Her winking is akin to a bolt of lightning
Her laughter is tricky and heart-ravishing

Her locks are serpents guarding her beauty's treasure
Or like chains thrown around a ferocious prisoner

As she twitches her sword-like eyebrows
Lovers fall without being slaughtered

Her eyelashes are sharper than a lance
No one escapes from them unscathed

When they flicker with a slight motion
Many a heart is shattered to pieces

II

Her lovely locks circled around her cheeks
Like the serpents curling around a treasure

Her mole was a grain, her tresses a snare's loop
Trapping in it many a houri and fairy

Her coquettish eyes stirred up a commotion
Provocative, sharp and spilling blood

Her body made fun of the fairest jasmine
The eglantine blushed at the flush of her face

Her safflower-like eyes were brimming wine cups
Casting a gloom on all who stole a wink at her

A rosy face, hyacinth curls and cypress stature
In short, a hundred doomsdays for the heartsick

The girl was known by the name Layla
Some thought her a fairy, others a celestial being

Qais's wits went awry at the first sight
Engrossed in her, he forgot his lessons

Her image got etched in him like an inscription
Her presence in the school made him ill at ease

A complete hush fell on him as he gazed her face
'What's behind the beauty's form?' he wondered

In her absence he wept grievously
Layla had agitated his young heart

Both began to steal glances at each other
Love's flame had licked their young bodies

When together, they pored over the Quran's pages
And stole a few moments to exchange a word

For him, her face was the scripture's fresh page
Her skewed glances were the strokes of *jeem*

As love suddenly unveiled its visage to them
It made them drunk with the wine of longing

~

Vatsuns

~

1. *manne nãvith antan yār*[1]

Body and soul, I will keep adorned.
Friend, coax my love to come.

Keep my bower decked for you,
O you with a million names![2]
Like a doll decorated, I will wait on you.

My tulip gave the garden a slip.
Could I deck my love with garlands!
It blossomed for a while
then vanished suddenly,
enjoying a brief stint.

Who can lie by your side?
Could I hang my arms around you?
Who can awaken you from sleep,
or stick to you perpetually?

Love, do look back once
and grasp the meaning of my words.

Mahmud leaves with unfulfilled yearnings.
The world is but a vain fantasy.
Deep in the grave's pit he goes from here.

Friend, coax my love to come.

2. *katyu chuk nund bāney*[3]

Where are you? O Charmer of hearts!
Come, my love, come.

You have a fairy's face.
How majestic you will look
in golden robes!
But who, tell me, has held you spellbound?
Why did you slip away
setting my breast afire?
What's the secret of your grief and gall?

Away you stay from love's station
while longings surge within me.
I shall surely die this way.
This separation chips off my frame
and leaves me benumbed,
while your languid eyes torch me down.

Once we sat face to face,
held together by love's thrall.
That is a vain craving now.

Waiting, my eyes are drooping.
Why have you turned so cold?

Tonight, rise like the moon on the full.

If you arrive by the riverbank,
I will wash your bonny feet.
The brands caused by your parting
have still not faded.

Could I feast my eyes on
the spectacle of your beauty?
Your black curls and dark mole
are like stinging snakes
coiling around me most malignantly.

Let's us fill our cups with wine
and make garlands of roses.
For tomorrow or later
we shall surely die.

Come, Mahmud, cheer up.
Sound reason is your Lord's gift.
Think not of separation.
Come, my love, come.

4. *kyāh wani ādam yath yaksānas*[4]

How shall man explain this oneness?
He is here to behold Himself.[5]

Slowly this truth will dawn upon him:
He is one, has countless names.[6]
What can an ignorant one know of it?

The bazaar of beauty is on display.
Priceless is every curve and cut.[7]
You put a high price on my pearl![8]

Beyond the space, above the skies
is the believer's heart and the throne of God[9]
which steals a glimpse of the grandeur divine.

Immerse in the Quran's chapter of Oneness.[10]
He neither begets nor is begotten.
He provides sustenance to all.

The bulbul found his way to the garden.
The blooming rose delights his heart.[11]
The rose turns the autumn into spring.

The fearless moth rushes forth
to burn itself in the assembly's midst,
illumined by the consuming flame[12]

He became a Brahmin and entered the temple.
The ascetic's piety is befuddled.[13]
His love of idols hides his faith.

Mahmud is ready to lay his life
for him who receives the Bountiful's blessings.[14]
For this reason, he is pleased with God.
He is here to behold Himself.

7. *ān jān-e man jānān-e man*[15]

He who was my life and soul
left me crazed and fled.

Lured me into a tavern
made me drink cup after cup
squeezed all soberness from me
left me drunk and fled.

He combed his locks straight
and confounded the poor hyacinth
He, the lord of the celestial world,
left me crazed and fled.

Ah, that rose of my desire!
gracing a Chinese gallery.
I wish I could inscribe
What he did to me and fled!

My love, that Turkish archer,
let fly a barrage of love darts
I offered my head to them
He slew me and fled.[16]

Since his effulgence fell on me
I am lost to myself.
He made me a circling moth
of the dark night's candle and fled.

His eyes are drunk deep
and His gaze is fixed upon Himself.
No wonder the mirror is perplexed
He left me dazed and fled.[17]

His mole, a grain of black pepper,
brings scalding tears in my eyes.
I brought him from Indian plains
He made me cry and fled.[18]

How lovely are his eyes!
Like two pearls shining brightly
on a jewel from Badakhshan.[19]
He laughed at me and fled.

In the dimple-well of his chin
lies a drop of sweat like dew.
Like a houri taking a dip
He left me dry and fled.

O cypress swinging gracefully!
I clutch at your hem.
Stay only for a moment.
He fettered me and fled.[20]

I lured him into a secret chamber
with captivating tales,
and seated him on the royal carpet.
He concocted a ruse and fled.

I am struck hard by wonder
and rendered speechless.
How can I relate the story
of what he did and fled?

With his dark grain-like mole
and his swirling tresses,
like a Turkish curl
he tied me and fled.

With his bewitching eyes
he stole my heart.
I am drenched in shame to say:
He flirted with me and fled.

O love, Mahmud's heart is ever longing
and devoted to your visage.
In the garden of Sulaimān
he told me a tale
and fled.[21]

9. *bāl maray te hāl wanay tse*

I will die young.
So let me tell you my tale
Come, love, sit awhile.

Come, I will spread velvet sheets for you
and daub my body with ambergris.
Don't let grief eat into you.

Come to this youthful girl.
I will be gone soon.
My clayey frame will decay in earth.
Then, it will be too late!

Your apathy enflames my very being.
Alas, you thought me worthless
and let me be slighted by others!
Love's fire emits no flame, no smoke.

Where have you hidden yourself
letting my garden's bloom go waste?
Or are you enjoying a nap by a spring?

O handsome youth of fiery demeanour!
Seeing your beauteous form,
I have lost all sleep and rest.

You shot arrows from afar
and showed no mercy.

I offered my breast as a shield.

Your regal looks inspire awe.
O coquettish love, drunk with pride,
Why do you scorn sincere love?

Pray, do not shoot arrows
from your arched brows.
When you did so, I bared my breast
and had my heart riddled.

Mahmud misses you much.
Keep your word, O true of word,
and come to me today!
What else can one consumed by love ask?
Come, love, sit awhile.

10. *yād geyam nād dimay hāy matyo lo*

Something stirs up your memories
and makes me follow your steps.
What was behind, I want to ask,
beguiling me first and then putting me aside?

I am a wanderer now, slain by bashfulness
that comes from talking love.

Your constant thought wastes me away.
An innocent girl has borne stings of ridicule.

With all blandishments, I hankered after you
but all in vain.
Now I am like a jasmine decaying in its bloom.

When I was a budding girl, you abandoned me
and broke the vow of love.

A fickle lover though you are
yet, being away from you is
an unbearable agony.

Come to me armed with all you have
or else call me unto you.

Either you don't steal someone's heart
or having stolen it, you don't turn cold.

Mahmud's passion refuses to abate.
Find an excuse to come to him.

12. *astay astay bāg-e babar vathrāvas*

Gently, I will spread petals and leaves for him.
Go, my friend, bring him to me, gently.

One day he became cross and left.
If only I could remind him, my childhood love,
of his vow and make him see his tyranny.
Would he then soften a bit?

For him, I am sighing away my soul.

For him, I will bathe in saffron and camphor water.
Beg him to sit with me under the breezy shade of the
chinar.

Let my love not jeer at a hapless girl.
Bewitched by him who has a heart of stone
but for whose single glance I will deck myself
with roses and jasmines.

For that blithe lover, I would carve a throne and a
bed.
Waiting is a torment when one is decaying fast.
Like a jasmine garden, a fleeting summer is passing
over my youth.

By a gushing spring, I will lie in wait for my Nāgrāy[22]

See what happened to Farhād after Shīrīn[23]
He struck himself with his axe and died

How shall I deal with Fate's cunning?

See what befell Majnun in his pursuit of Layla.
He feigned blindness, lay prostrate before God
and kept looking for her in the plains of Najd.[24]

See what came over San'ān in his love for the Hindu girl.[25]
He wore a pagan thread and took to keeping her swine.

He used to boast, we know, of seven thousand
disciples at his command.

What does it profit me to have pearls, necklaces and
tinkering hems?
What good are music, kohl and all other ornaments?
Why should I adorn myself, if he is not pleased?

O you who are drunk, don't race away from my
street.
You who have sneaked like a thief and robbed my
senses.

To God alone can Mahmud relate his woes!
Go, my friend, bring him to me, gently.

13. *lejim phulyah yāvneni hiye lolo*

My youth's jasmine is in full bloom today.
But once withered, it won't return.

Rise, O heedless one, shake off your slumber.
Search all six dimensions for your love who
leaves no trace behind.[26]

Rise early and pay obeisance to your Lord.
Servitude means humbling yourself.
'Indeed, You are our Lord' will ring again
in your ears.[27]

Go to Achabal and spruce yourself.
A boat awaits you at Khanabal.[28]

Who can drain death's cup so deep?

Whether we wear velvet, satin or brocade
it is dust that will be our last bedding
where our delicate bodies will be roughed up
and bruised.

Lady, don't gloat like Nimrod.[29]
Plenty like you have come here and gone.
Shaddād and Hātim Tay too came and went.[30]

Mahmud, regard the world as a vain enterprise
that we shall leave empty-handed one day.
But keep the spark of hope alive.

20. *ābas andar naqshāh zānto*

Look upon life as an image
writ in water
or a dreamy thought, my dear love!

Let us go for a boat ride in Tel Bal
O you decked with pearl necklaces!

Shalimar garden is blooming.
I beg you to meet me there.

Nishat garden is graced with freshness
Come, let's stay at Sona Lank.[31]

I saw you loitering with my rivals
Pray, do not blast me with envy!
Your curled locks I descried from afar.
These jet-black curls look like snakes.

Love, I am sighing away my soul
as serpents have coiled around me.
Your absence eats into me.
You didn't ask after me!

Pining for you,
my heart is branded.
This mole is of unmatched beauty.
I am caught in the snare of your love.

My young heart had nurtured
a desire of meeting you.
Mahmud still waits for the day
when you will show up.

21. *yine bu sare hā tī pyom sare nuy*

I am beset with a daunting task.
I was indeed better off dead![32]

Collect something for the journey ahead.
Union fulfils heart's desire.
I have to brave the fiercest storm!
I was indeed better off dead!

The heart must proclaim God's Oneness.
The chaste body will meet the Beloved.
Though I am torn to shreds,
I must endure the pain.
I was indeed better off dead!

What does this exultation avail me?
Being born, I am walking towards death.
The worry lacerates by flesh and bones.
I was indeed better off dead!

Today or tomorrow death will surely come.
I know not how I will give up my soul.
I have to cross a rough river in a trembling
palanquin[33]
I was indeed better off dead!

But once born why should you fear death?
Rise and recite, 'Everything shall perish.'[34]
Mahmud, spend your youth to realize this truth.
I was indeed better off dead!

23. *mati sorān ām yāvun ye*

My youth is withering away fast.
He keeps fanning my love's flame.

Find a seasoned guide
who reveals the great secret to you.[35]
Unguided, you will be stranded.

God made Adam's mould from clay.
And ordered the spirit to go inside.
He promised him another exit.[36]

In the smithy the billows are at work,
transmuting iron into gold.
Step on the touchstone
and separate the dross from purity.[37]

Love's river is deeper than I thought.
Without a bridge or a boat to sail across.
It is a river worth fathoming.

Pearls are genuine and counterfeit too.
They don't fetch the same price.
Go in search of a royal pearl.
You will know it when you find one.

If you leave for the market
with an empty pocket,
you will buy nothing except ridicule.[38]

One day you will return home.
O heedless man, wake up.
Make provisions for the journey ahead.

My days of youth are rolling by.
I am a shrivelled pomegranate flower.
The autumn gale has barged into my garden.

Mahmud, reckon with your loneliness.
Duality is an unbearable burden.[39]
It's time to fathom God's oneness.
He keeps fanning my love's flame.

24. *mo roz ghāfil bey khabar*

Live not the life of a heedless man.
This clayey frame will crumble soon.[40]

A single glance from the angel of death.
And eyes turn blind, ears deaf.
There is no escape from this inevitability.

When they place me in my grave
The two appointed angels will question me.
'O stone-hearted man what if the earth squeezes you?'

As they unfold the record of my deeds.
Lo, my sins are many, they will rise in heaps!
I alone will bear their burden!

A hundred and twenty-four thousand messengers
All of whom were warners to the mankind.
May my life be their sacrifice![41]
Our great master returned from the heavens.[42]

O heedless soul, catch up with the caravan.
When will you finish such a long journey?
And when will news from there reach here?

When the doors of Paradise are thrown open
God will leave out none.[43]
Mahmud says this with utmost confidence.
This clayey frame will crumble soon!

30. *braem dith tsolum tay tohi mā dyunthvan*[44]

Friends, did you see him who beguiled me
and slipped away?
He whose elegant stature compares with
a lofty box tree.

He showed his bright face
and stole my heart, swinging his earrings.

I left home to persuade him.
Alas, he did not regard me with favour!
Someone beseech him softly
so that he relents.
My quest for him has been a long one.

The fire of absence has reduced me to ash.
Could I meet him somewhere?
Dressed in rags, I roamed several ports
hoping to catch his glimpse.
How I wish he showed up once
and prevented my jasmine body from decaying!

If only I knew the way
I would run after him
and see where he has hidden himself.
I would hide somewhere to catch him unawares
and lay my plea before him.

My great desire is to clutch at his hem
and say, 'Resolve my love's dilemma'.

The day of Eid is come.
How I wish I could send him greetings
and laments of my heart too!

Come, sweet-voiced fairies, let's sing and dance
somewhere in the dense shade of a grove.
And flit from branch to branch like nightingales.
My saffron bowls, filled for his sake, are lying waste.

Wasted too are all my blandishments.
If perchance he visits me,
I will welcome him with a host of maids.
All draped in velvet and brocade.

As to myself, I will rub ash on my body
and set on his trail like a hermit,
stealthily watching his every step.

In a dream he showed me his radiant cheek
and scorched my heart with love's fire.
I saw him in full splendour
like a glowing moon
throwing a flood of radiance around
or like Yusuf whose presence in
Egypt's market lit it up
and made the sun slink into concealment.[45]

Come, dear, rescue me.
Let me not waste away.

He titillated me and made off.
Which rival of mine told him tales?
The agony within lies pent up.
Who is there I could share that with?

Mahmud craves for someone who
can guide him in the path of love.

32. *ker tham manz woandas jāy*

You carved a niche in my heart
This longing will not wane!

What's my body now?
A blazing pan of love.
That chars my aching heart.
Though reduced to ashes
I uttered no complaint.
Your thoughts kept me going!

These deadly serpentine tresses.
Oh, do not flaunt them so!
Life's hope hinges on you.
My heart is suffused with your love!

To the altar of your godly frame
from head to foot
I will offer nosegays.
Serve you as a slave
and wait on you to catch a glimpse.
To me you are unforgettable!

From the bows of your arched eyebrows
shoot not the darts of piercing eyelashes.
My heart is stabbed and bleeds.
I am transfixed by your memories!

May you live long like Ruma Rishi![46]
This love too shall abide.
What if I nurture unfulfilled cravings?
I live thinking ever of your love!

Were you to hear my sorry tale
my petition would be granted.
One glimpse of you will calm my eyes.
Oh, how I cherish your memories!

I am wasting away!
Cease this murderous toying.
Salvage me from the frowns of fortune
and redeem my soul.
To forget you is beyond me!

From the cups of china, drink a beverage.
We are to die someday.
What for were we born then?
This pining shall never abate!

We have not come here to stay.
The earth will devour us soon.
And once dead, we will turn to dust.
My longing heart knows no peace!

My seething passion brooks no silence
and the pain dwindles not a bit.
Come and play your lute and rebeck.
Your memories are etched into my soul!

Ask yourself—what brought us here?
And why Mahmud turned insane?
Slight me not with such heedlessness.
This longing will not wane!

33. *roshe waolo pōsh ho bo lāgay*

Come secretly, I will deck myself with flowers.
Give me an ear, I will relate my woes.

I will fix my gaze on your love's garden.
Wherever you bloom, I will be there.
For I have pledged myself to you.

Since you combed your locks
envy has thrown hyacinths into shambles.
My sorry state you know well.
I need not tell:
Body and soul, I am in distress.

Your narcissi are drunk on wine.
Abashed and downcast
these languorous eyes have slain
the gazelles in the jungle.

You stabbed me with love's dagger
and ripped this heart to shreds.
Now it knows no comfort,
wounded as it is by your fatal blow.

You put yourself on display
and reserve your veiling for me.
Love's feverish ardour consumes me.
I am a jasmine withered away.

I have no strength to bear it any longer.
Only laments can soar from Mahmud's soul!

34. *yas māshoq dake dith tsale nay*

He whose beloved spurns him
His wounds are not healed.

Though the gardens be in bloom
and others enjoy boat rides
and countless bounties be placed before him.
His wounds are not healed.

His feet are blistered with ceaseless running
searching for his love at every door.
Though he be draped in silk and velvet
His wounds are not healed.

When the bonded slaves serve their term
they receive the tidings of freedom.
But who is caught in love's snare
His wounds are not healed.

Grief weighs down the box tree.
Farhād dug out several canals.
Yet he could not meet his love.
His wounds were not healed.[47]

The lady from Ād tried her luck
at buying the angelic Yusuf.[48]
Indeed, she had lost her wits.
The axe of love chopped her to pieces.
Her wounds were not healed.

If you wash the feet of the love-afflicted one
He will feel it like scalding.
Nothing can soothe or cool them.
His wounds will not be healed.

How can a gathering of mirth
lift up the spirits of him whose
bones are eaten by the sorrow of love?

When hyacinth curls are tossed wildly
Even the pious Sādi is chained.[49]
No one has escaped that whirlpool.

When the silver pillars of the mirror-house tremble
You will say: 'If only I had heeded before!'[50]
When love's seething unsettles one's senses
Then the wounds are not healed.

Mahmud, only there will they be healed.
For they are the wounds of love.
One who holds back himself
His wounds will not be healed.[51]

37. *kar sa myon nyāy andey*

When will you end my predicament?
My lovely, charming sweetheart!

I searched for you everywhere
but never had a glimpse of you.
O love, boasting constancy!
How I wish I had you in front of me!
My lovely, charming sweetheart!

Brutal—yet you are my only treasure.
When the night falls, come to me
and secretly unveil yourself.
My lovely, charming sweetheart!

My rivals in love are taunting me.
O winged Cupid, ever flitting!
Since long I have been wailing.
My lovely, charming sweetheart!

You laid a trap for my heart and soul.
Is there more I owe you?
Only if you come can I gather myself.
My lovely, charming sweetheart!

Why do you stay shy of me
when I want you so badly?
Alas, I am caught in Fate's snare!
My lovely, charming sweetheart!

My heart is ruined, no, devastated!
Wine-drinker, you have got me drunk.
Now come, enjoy my garden's bloom.
My lovely, charming sweetheart!

Why have you plunged me in gloom?
O throat-decking pearl necklace!
If I could have you about my throat once!
My lovely, charming sweetheart!

Your search took me to the frontiers.
Why are you still scarring me?
Parted from you, I have passed my hours crying.
My lovely, charming sweetheart!

Here comes poor Mahmud,
begging an irresistible you!
Give him an ear, for God's sake!
My lovely, charming sweetheart!

39. *pāne myāne ghāfil anay*[52]

My blind heedless self.
Pity, you could not
pick your beloved sitting
in the midst of your eye![53]

I am chastised by love's woe.
It has wracked my body
tearing it apart bit by bit.

Heart's passion dwindles
like a withering rose.
A moment's distraction and
only the thorn is left behind.
The bulbul then vainly looks about, wailing.[54]

When the empty cage will collapse
and the bird lose its wits[55]
It will be too late to heed then.

When love's malady seeps within
all busyness is paralysed.
Only the sufferer knows its ache.

Look around in all directions.
Behold the godly light
shining everywhere.
Only that which I earned is mine.[56]

Why have you abandoned your journey halfway?
Don't leave your pursuit unfinished.
What is obscure here will be manifest there.[57]

He who fathoms the truth of his self
becomes averse to the daily business.
For he beholds his love before him.

When Mahmud's passion grew intense
he brought his case before his Lord.
Who else would he have turned to?

Pity, he could not pick his beloved
sitting in the midst of his eye!

45. *soz diluk be kyāh wanay*

My heart's smouldering is a tale
worth listening.
Sit a while and lend me your ear.

O Cupid, donned in a glamorous robe!
You slipped away at dusk
and haven't returned since.
Away from you my body is melting away.
And my days are spent crying.

You are away near border gypsies.
Steal a moment to see me somewhere.

Why do you turn a deaf ear?
The days of youth will slip away fast.
And soon the messenger will come for us.[58]
What good is it being born?

Stop and sit for a moment with me.
Shun your ego and remember that
youth is an illusion.

Like a candle burning ceaselessly
my young body too burns.

Love's sickness afflicts guileless people like me.
Come now, it is not too late yet.

50. *chāni amāre gous beytābo*

Pining for you, I have lost all repose.
O moon, I miss you sorely!

Your eyes have drunk deep.
Give me a look without ire.
I sipped your wine and was ruined.

Your cheeks have stolen flush from the roses.
Reveal yourself in a sudden flash.
Throw off this veil from your visage.

Your body shines like quicksilver.
Now a raging fire, now a sweeping torrent.
Smitten with it, I am neither alive nor dead.
O moon, I miss you sorely!

51. *damāh beh mey bronh kani*[59]

A Paean to Love

Sit for a while before me.
Come, O Love, listen to this tale.

You were the first to arrive.
I heard you come.
With you arrived the Emperor.
I long for the day of union with you.[60]

What meets the eye here
will reveal its truth there.[61]
Since you were born, you lord over time
You encompass days and years.

Hu, the primeval word, blends with the spirit
Even as the soul blends with the body.
I am caught between the two![62]

You brought Yusuf from Canaan.
You robbed Zulaykha of her senses.
How many lost their youth after you!

Heaven's throne can't bear your weight.
On the earth you hold sway.
You grace all places, high and low.

Sometime you came tied to Attributes.
At times as a king draped in brocade.
You play the lover and the beloved.[63]

The reed-flute raises laments and wails:
'My heart is riddled in absence.
Torn from my roots, I keep crying.'

Farhād, they say, dug out a stream.
'Shīrīn, show me a glimpse, please!
I will bring forth a stream, singing sad songs!'

Shīrīn said, 'I shall be pleased.'
Her word made him cleave the rocks.
But disaster struck before he could see her.

I have a word of wisdom to share.
They pricked a vein of Layla for blood.
But it was Majnun who bled
from every vein without a lancet's prick.
Every drop fell on ground inscribing
Layla's name.[64]

Sheikh San'ān was effaced
when Rome's Hindu girl appeared to him.
Love's fervour made him tend her swine.
He burnt the holy book and his robe
and rehearsed the lesson of love.
Remember, appearance is never bereft of the
Essence.[65]

Candle, you will not burn endlessly.
It takes a moment for the moth to burn up.
Circling around you, he immolates himself.
Without heaving a sigh, he embraces death.
Without divulging the secret, he sends out a shriek.[66]

How many have perished at your altar!

You made Mansur cry, 'I am the Truth'.
You made him disclose the secret.
You became the seer and the seen.[67]

Let no one be rent from their love.
Let separation be no body's fate.

The grave is a place of utter ruin.
You need someone to bring news from there.
Die unto love to irradiate your being.[68]

Mahmud, without the wine of love
there is no way to inebriation.
And nothing will avail
without the battering of the tavern.

68. *bar buke āyas wane hā khodāyas*

To God I will confide the constriction of my heart.
Would that my love relents a little!

I was fated to desert my kin.[69]
But he thought it disgraceful to come to me.
Now I am caught in Fate's snare.
Would that my love relents a little!

I set out to searching for flowers in winter.
Looking for him my bright day was blighted with
darkness.

I will pluck a hair string to raise a note.
Love's calamity is an overwhelming affair.
How shall Mahmud tackle its predicament?
Would that my love relents a little!

69. *yane yāre chuhom tsetas pevān*

Remembering you, my love, brings
a stream of tears in its train.

Beauty, you broke with me
and didn't miss me ever.
There is no cure for the affliction
wrought by you.

Your beaming chin snatches my senses.
Why do you make me dizzy?

Whose wine cups are you draining?
O you, drunk with musky wine![70]

How can I be merry when
the pain of love frets my heart
and I can only weep?
Love's raging fire melts my marrow.

Its morbid fever scorches my liver.
I languish in despair.
Give me a cure.

Love, I keep calling you.
Friends, I am forlorn.

I pass my nights and days in vigil
staring at the stars and the moon.

Mahmud's aching heart knows no respite.
Whose praise, O trickster, will he sing now?

88. *yūt kya bosh chuy yāvnun josh chuy*

So puffed up with youth's fervour
and graces!
O ear-decking pearl, come to me.

Though I have no heart to have you face to face,
Yet, O love with crystal eyes, come to me.

On your face, soft as a lotus petal,
a bead of sweat shines like a dewdrop.
O love with dagger-like eyebrows, come to me.

My breast craves your soothing touch
and I pine for a word or two with you.

A dagger protrudes from your silvery brow
and viper-shaped tresses adorn your crown.[71]

You keep simmering my heart's ardour,
O love, slinking away with graceful motions!

How I long to rock you inside my breast
and put a price on you in the jewel market![72]

I am held fast by the chains
of your tresses around my neck.

Taken by your charms,
I am love's unhappy victim.
Show your face once, O my heart's calamity!

O beauty, you have left your lovers restive.
Wake up from your sleep, come to me.

One named Mahmud harbours your desire.
Listen to the plea he has written for you.

89. *yīna sōn dobāre lolo*

Would he come again to me
and drain the brimming cups?

I would con his face like the scripture's page
For my heart is broken into thirty pieces![73]

The faithless one swore allegiance there
and now he turns haughty, unresponsive.[74]

Himself colourless, yet draped in myriad colours
I searched for Him in plains and hills.[75]

Don't be proud of your languid eyes.
I will feign sickness to outdo them.

At dusk, I set out to look for him.
That god of love with a moon-like face.

In the garb of a hermit in retreat
Mahmud roams the streets and bazaars.

92. shīn zan gaejthas hā jōyan laejthas

You melt me like snow
and send me adrift in gushing streams.
Your love, a midsummer's blazing sun.

Hear me out.
I bring you my entreaties!
Love, let my head be a sacrifice unto your feet.

Friend, this longing is a searing force.
Come quietly and save me from losing my wits.

On the banks of Tel Bal, my moon will be rid of its
eclipse.[76]
And the garden of my youth will bloom again.

Mahmud Gāmi pleads with you.
Love, he pledges his head to you.

104. *chāni bar tal rāweym hā raetsi*

Countless nights passed
as I sat by your door, calling.
Didn't my call reach you?

Of crimson cups and yellow petals
I am a jasmine of Paradise.
Long is the wait till Judgement Day
Didn't my call reach you?

To serve you selflessly like a maid
was a desire my heart nourished.
But you showed me only apathy.
Now they call me Lalla, the crazed one.
Didn't my call reach you?

In earnest hope Mahmud would rehearse
the tale of love.
If only you lend him an ear.

Alas, how many pretty faces turn to dust!
Didn't my call reach you?

Nazms

~

1. Põmpir Nāmah

The Moth's Tale[77]

The moth has great fame
as the lover with a fiery soul.
Glimpsing the candle, his heart-kindler,
he sets himself aflame.

One day, some flies pestered him.
'Tell us your love's secret.
Give us a name or a clue, at least.

Who has stolen your heart?
What have your eyes seen?'

The moth wailed, raised lamentation
and gave a loud shriek.

'I am a moth driven crazy by love.
My anguish defies description.
He only knows who suffers love's seething pain.'

He went on:
'Fetch a burning candle emitting light
and regard it with discerning eyes.'

The flies searched for a candle frantically
and found one burning alone.
They pledged their love
and fluttered around its flame.
But flinched from flinging themselves into
its devouring fire.

Alas, for those who set out in earnest
but leave the journey half-way!
Such stragglers only bring
shame to the lovers.

And then the moth rushed to the flame
and burnt himself up,
without a sob, a cry or a complaint.
He did the lovers proud.

Truth and deception fell apart.
The sage had proved his point.
Fire, light and the lover's soul
all fell into a unity.

Wonderstruck, they asked the moth:
'What made you embrace the flame?

What great promise did you keep
jumping foolishly in the fire?'

So, he told the tale of his coming of age.

'He who feeds on himself learns the inner secret.
Inside the flame I saw the Beloved
busy in self-display.
Instantly, I ran to Him.
And my fiery anguish turned into
a rose garden's bliss.

His radiance I descried from afar.
Now I understand why
the *Tūr* was blown away
in a single flash.'[78]

Tears streamed down the candle's face too.
They asked, 'O faithful friend,
what conflagration rose from your heart
to burn down your stately frame?'

He replied:
'I invoke this verse as a witness to my state:
We are nearer to him than his jugular vein.[79]
And don't forget this one:
He is with you wherever you are.[80]

Sit among candle-like hearts
to make your own soft like wax.
And get the answers to your being's puzzle.'[81]

How can the blind see in darkness
the heart's blooming rose?
Only the moth and the candle know
love's secret.
Like the bulbul knows the rose.

You are a veil to yourself.
Rise and move away.
Do not stay outside.
Go inside and learn the truth.

To live in darkness
is unbecoming of a lover.
A true seeker keeps his eye
on the longed-for goal.

Alas, no one has the courage of the moth!
And no one nears what he conquers with ease.

Mahmud, dying for the Friend is the highest bliss.
One who dies for love dies the death of a martyr.[82]

2. Tamsīl-e Ādam

The Parable of Man[83]

I inquired of the bubble
the parable of man:
'Reveller, how do you stay alive in water?'

'Clutch at the rope of contemplation.
Pull at the pulley of remembrance.[84]
Your soul's wheel will whirl in a dance
like it's pulled with a rope.
Let no joy or dream waylay you.'

I asked a craftsman the secret of his craft:

'Tie your heart to a hook and burn like a kebab
which becomes the tastier the more it burns.'

All seekers pursue their goals.
The pedant waxes eloquent through the bookish lore
while trifles occupy the heedless man.[85]

The drinker alone is witness to wine's potency.
While the ascetic labours to pile up rewards,
the true lover has no fear of love's torment.[86]

When out of love, the Lover blew,
the bubble was born.
He blew again,
it mingled with water.
What has perished?
What left for reckoning?[87]

Tear off the veil and look inside.
You will find God and his Prophet together.[88]
Take lead, fear not fury or punishment.

A boat in the water and water in the boat.
Such is the likeness of God and his Prophet.
The Prophet in turn consorts with his companions.[89]

Every form has a meaning.
And no dream is without an explanation.
The rose is one with its fragrance.
The veil hides nothing from he who attains union.

Love's great puzzle has no answer.
But if its meaning you ever fathom,
you get yourself counted then.

When you reach the Kāba's centre
which way do you turn your face to kneel?[90]

My restless soul craves longingly
to see the ray one with the sun?[91]

Mahmud Gāmi inquired of the bubble
'Reveller, how do you stay alive in water?'

3. Kalewāl

Wine Server

Would that I could lay down my head
for that wine server
that thief of wits

who beguiled me with a single trick
and made me drunk
on a heady wine!

His earthen cup
more fragrant than the perfume
infuses sweetness into me.
He pours the wine of gnosis[92]
into the cup.
And I drink it up.

My love has deserted me
making me heart-forlorn.
I wonder why?
If only I knew what has annoyed him!

He has snatched my felicity.
Could I grab him by his collar,
or follow his steps wherever he goes
or throw my arms around his neck?

My youth has gone waste.
It's past redemption.
My Nāgrāy, that tantalizer
enticed and kept his Hīmāl teetering on the edge.[93]

He has retired to a mountain
like a hermit
making me a wanderer.
I, who was once a cheerful girl.

The lover sits expectantly
to have a glimpse of that beauty.
Surely, the lovers' meeting will take place
and the sea of union will surge.

This mole, this shapely down,
and these snare-like curls!
What lover can resist their charm?

The curling tresses will grow
and attain to their desire.
Like the black slave, Bilāl.[94]

Chanter of God's names,
Hold your breath.
Cleanse your heart-mirror of rust,
and the truth will dawn on you.

Gaining grit,
a weakling turns mighty.
Mountains shudder
when a man of grit
takes to the wilderness.[95]

Grit tells the lion from the jackal.
To have this grit
He passed me through tough penance.
A gem can only be quarried from the hard rock.

Grit runs through the northern wind
giving it a name and fame
to shake the mountains.

The crooked letter *dāl*
bows to the straight *alif*[96]

It is ages since my love left me.

When *hay* got in between
alif and *dāl,*
Who could tell
who bowed to whom?[97]
These are the fruits of
ecstasy and rapture.

How much more will
Mahmud put up with love's chronic sorrow?
His heart is lacerated now.
Who has the heart to hear his tale?

~

4. Pāne Myāney . . .

My Dear Self, Remember Death

My dear self, O ignorant one
Know that the world is a vale of tears.

Adam, who was our first ancestor
Was also the first to taste death.
His clayey body mingled with dust.

The Prophet Nooh too bewailed
When his soul and body were rent apart.
His thousand years seemed a moment.[98]

Ibrāhīm, known as the 'friend of God'[99]
The only man death might have spared.
But it came and took him away.

King Yusuf, the glorious one![100]
He too surrendered his dear life.
How many were devastated by his death?

Dāwood, a prophet with heavenly voice.[101]
See, he too perished in the end.
Death brought him down like all others.

Sulaimān, the owner of the flying throne[102]
Ruled at one time, where is he now?
Laid desolate by the chilling death.

Yahya who used to say[103]
'What can death do to me?'
Died one day, uttering a cry.

Moosa, a prophet who conversed with God[104]
Entered his grave with a robust body.
Though he was gifted with a sweet tongue.

Plato, the Greek, and Luqmān, the sage[105]
Who can match their wisdom?
When death approached, they lost their wits.

Alexander, the world conqueror[106]
Tried to find death's cure.
But death, he learnt, has no cure.

Idrīs and Isa are stationed on the sky.[107]
Khizr and Ilyās are here on the earth.[108]
The latter two try to evade death.

The last messenger of God, Muhammad.
It was no wonder if he were immortal.
He too submitted to the call of death.

His four close friends[109]
Wished for death while living.
But when in death throes, they sought an escape.

Saints and men of highest station
Feared the last reckoning.
The wealthy left empty-handed.

In the grave the two angels are lying in wait[110]
To throw the sinners in a burning pit.
How can you escape, O weakling?

If you are a true believer
And know your faith well
Your path ahead will be easy.

Your place in the Paradise you will see.
You will be served all delicious dishes.
Houris and keepers of Paradise will welcome you.

And one who leaves this world without faith
Will know the price he will pay.
Remorse and sorrow will be his lot.

The living mix with the living.
The dead blend with the dead.
Once there, all will act as strangers.

Eyes, ears, limbs and all
Are witness to all your acts.[111]
They will relate all good and evil.

No one carries your burden here.
Carry something for yourself.
Forgetting death is a great folly.

O reveller, don't feign to be drunk.
Wake up from your idle slumber.
Don't rely on the thing called life.

Your diminishing strength is a sign of death.
Your greying hair a signal too.
Your heart is stony still, what a pity!

Illness and pain are but ploys of death.
Look, where they all lead to.
Speechless are all humans before it.

When the angel of death will show up
You will not escape his stinging breath.
All noise and levity will turn to air.

Your kith and kith will carry you, crying.
But you will not return home at dusk.
No one can return from that country.

Others will devour your wealth.
Alone you will answer there.
Soon you will be forgotten here.

On a wooden plank they will wash me.
How can the world satiate my eyes?
O stony heart, I fear your disgrace.

You pride yourself on graceful speech?
God grant you His grace.
Or else you will live to rue.

How many youths has death devoured!
All nurtured by the parental love.
How many homes were laid desolate!

Fathers, mothers, brothers and sisters.
Dearest sons and daughters lovable.
See, the caravan keeps moving.

The spectacle of death ever
appears before your eyes.

How can you then forget it?
Not once do you reflect on this.

Recite: 'All is bound to perish.'[112]
Only God shall remain.
Hear me, take Him for a friend.

O Mahmud, you feeble soul!
Keep God ever in your heart.
Sow today to reap tomorrow.
Know that the world is a vale of tears.

Masnavis

~

1. Khusrau Shīrīn

Khusrau hears about Shīrīn from his confidante
Shāpur and sets out to meet her.

Praise be to Him who created life
Heaven, the earth, love and knowledge

Next, countless blessings be on Muhammad
His august companions and noble family[113]

A thousand eulogies for his four friends[114]
The four strong pillars of his true faith

Ovations offered, now listen to my words
A love tale of Shīrīn, Khusrau and Farhād[115]

Nizāmi says so; we take him for his word
Khusrau was a cousin of Anushirwān[116]

Bubbling with youth and unsurpassed elegance
No less charming than the legendary Jamshīd[117]

At fourteen, he had a heart full of desire
He rose on the sky as a full bright moon

In manners sublime, noble and refined
The prince outmatched Cyrus and Kaiqabād[118]

One day he embarked on a hunting expedition
While a horse of his strayed into a paddy field

The king learnt this and reached the spot
And gave his son a sound bashing

Now the prince was terribly upset
His friends tried to cheer him up

He had a close confidant named Shāpur
Privy to his closely guarded secrets

He passed him a piece of information
About a queen ruling over Armān

'She's known to all as Mihīn Bānu
She runs her kingdom flawlessly

She has a niece, extremely dear to her
No less than a houri come from heaven

In stature she compares with a swinging cypress
Her silvery forearms are like box tree's boughs

Black dense hair covers her crown
So lovely, it looks like a dove's nest

The line splitting her ambergris hair
Gleams wondrously like a Chinese stream

A gold-embroidered cap that graces her head
Looks very elegant on the scented tresses

Call her a bright sun piercing through darkness
Or a pinkish-yellow rose blooming among lilies

Her swinging tresses scattered on her back
Like captivating nooses for the onlookers

When she stands upright her tresses fall straight
Their length compares with a life, lovers long for

Between her arched eyebrows and dagger-shaped
locks
There is whiteness like in the middle of a jasmine

Amidst the sandalwood-coloured forehead
The elegant brows appear as bloodied swords

Her forehead reflects bright divine light
What words can describe its refulgence?

So graceful is the medal on her brow
It looks like the midday's glowing sun

The mole between her two eyebrows
Looks like the dot on the letter *ghain*[119]

A sweet-scented mole betwixt her brows
Looks like a kingfisher darting through air

Or like a Negro with arms outstretched
About to pounce on a female deer

Her two enticing eyes are like those of a gazelle
Is she a ruthless sorcerer or a fretful sweetheart?

If perchance gazelles catch a glimpse of her
The kohl-rimmed eyes leave them stunned

Since those eyes have bewitched the gazelles
They have hidden themselves in the forests

Those eyes have made the narcissus sick
Its head has dropped down in shame

Those eyes are like two springs of wine
Her coquettishness too thrills like wine

Her winking is akin to a bolt of lightning
Her laughter is tricky and heart-ravishing

Her locks are serpents guarding her beauty's treasure
Or like chains thrown round a ferocious prisoner

As she twitches her sword-like eyebrows
Lovers fall without being slaughtered

Her eyelashes are sharper than a lance
No one escapes from them unscathed

If they flicker with a slight motion
Stony hearts too will shatter to pieces

Listen, if you may, to a subtle point
Black hearts come out baked from fire

How elegant looks the mole on her cheek!
No less than a snare for the poor lovers

Amidst the tresses, this mole stands unique
A sprightly gazelle jumping freely around

It looks splendid on her beautiful face
Like an Abyssinian prince sitting in a garden

The black mole adorns her rosy cheek
Like the black stone adorns the Kāba[120]

Like a speck on the pomegranate leaf
Or a black pepper seed in a blazing fire

Because of her, the tulip's heart is branded
Because of her, the wild rue ignites itself

Turning right and left, she tantalizes all men
Her graceful hands are a boon to the anguished

Listen carefully to what I say now
Beautiful earrings adorn her ears

Seven pearls hang down her each earlobe
Like seven sparkling Rishis risen from sulking

You can descry her earrings from afar
Twinkling like stars in dense darkness

Her shining, dangling eardrops
Make the restless more restive

Her ruby-red lips outshine all jewels
Her speech puts eloquence to shame

Her lips are as red as chewed betel leaves
Or is their redness due to our blood stains?

Her teeth are pearls strung in her mouth
Or are they dewdrops on tulip leaves?

Her laughter lights up the black night
Hail the two pearl strings shining thus![121]

Her nose looks like a flashing silvery dagger
Her mouth a narrow bud on the arch of *meem*[122]

Below the lips sits the round chin
Like a silver apple cleft in two

In vain is the search for calm here
A well lies beside a whirlpool here

The chin has a well, or is it a cavern of grief?
A paradisical pool or the Zamzam well?[123]

The chin decorated by a breathtaking dimple
A crow among jasmines or Hāroot in the well[124]

Her white neck drives the camphor candle to envy
It burns itself: 'How can I match such refulgence?'

That neck dwarfs the long ones of the swans
Before her stature, the cypress falls to its feet

Gazelles despair at a glimpse of that neck
Hyacinths are shamed as she unveils her locks

Her chest is brighter than the Aleppo mirror[125]
How lucky the man who may recline on it?

A bed of jasmines bruises her soft body
And makes her cry like a raining cloud

Her dome-shaped breasts are shields on her chest
Racking the nerves of those who may gaze on them

Like two silver bowls filled with creamy milk
Or two pomegranates burgeoning elegantly

Her soft delicate body emits radiance
The queen graces the lustrous throne

Princes long listlessly to see her from afar
Disheartened, how many eat a humble pie!

Her fragrance beats that of the musk-deer
Chastity's mantle covers her from the navel to feet

Ankles above, her limbs are like ivory towers
Below the waist are peerless silvery mounds

There lies an unpierced pearl yet to see a diamond
God has made self-restraint her supreme virtue

She is lovelier than my words can convey
Her name is Shīrīn, the sweet one'[126]

This account made Khusrau's heart restless
'Shāpur, not a drop of water till I have her'!

He ordered Shāpur to find a way to her
And fetch her for him come what may

~

Shāpur goes to meet Shīrīn in disguise, draws a portrait of Khusrau. Shīrīn falls in love with the portrait and decides to meet him.

Obeying the king's command, Shāpur set off
Reached Armān and hid in a flower-stack

He drew Khusrau's portrait on a paper
And took it secretly to Shīrīn's garden

He hung it on a tree near a spring
And waited for Shīrīn to come

The dawn flowered with the plaints of bulbuls
The spotless tulip too bloomed by then

Then Shīrīn made her joyful entry
Her joy could cure the sick of their illness

A fairy so charming among humans
Her presence made their hearts throb

With her friends she was sauntering there
And capturing lions with her gazelle-like eyes

Fairies and houries were at her service[127]
Busy in making fresh garlands for her

The air was filled with song and music
All were intoxicated by the wine of love

Shīrīn got drunk and drenched in sweat
Past soberness, yet still sharp of sight

She saw a beautiful portrait hanging by a tree
'Is that an angel, fairy or a heavenly face?'

The moment she saw it she fainted
Her crimson face turned saffron pale

The attendants rushed to revive her
Pleaded with her to reveal her ailment

She moaned, 'Oh, tell me who's he
A fairy, a human, or something else?

Who has drawn this breathtaking portrait?
Didn't he fall in love with what he drew?

I am yet to see a more handsome face
Would that this portrait came to life!

No one but him do I desire for myself
My heart inclines to no one except him

Alas, I am undone; friends, rescue me!
Pray to God to remove my moon's eclipse

Look for some old fakir to give me a clue
Has anyone ever seen a man like him?'

Shāpur disguised himself as a fakir
His ashen glow was just perfect

Shīrīn saw him and hurried alone
Showed him the portrait in her hand

'My lord,' she cried falling to his feet
'Have you ever seen this man?'

For a while the fakir feigned indifference
Then seeing her alone he made up his mind

He softly raised his head sunk in his knees
'Ah, this is Khusrau, the legendary man

A prince from the line of Anushirwān the Just
Look closely, this is his portrait

I reveal my secret, he saw you in a dream
Since then, he is yearning for you

He sent me to you to carry his message
Here is my proof, his royal signet ring

He is in Madāin, waiting anxiously
Or maybe, already on his way here'

Shīrīn and Shāpur thanked each other
Her bitter grief changed into sweet bliss

Shāpur so described Khusrau's person
Shīrīn was quickly won by his charms

She asked Shāpur to get ready
For the journey to the city of love

'Come Shāpur, accompany me to him
I have other passionate suitors in wait

You are my guide, a keeper of my secrets
Take me to him who has sent you here'

Shāpur said, 'Time has come, rise
Ride your horse Shabdīz, I will follow

You have to be a hunter after a game
I will follow your tracks closely behind

Take this ring of mine as a sign
And show it to him as you arrive'

She hardly waited for Shāpur to finish
Mounted her horse Shabdīz and was off

Soon she was negotiating rugged hills
And lost her way in the trackless sands

Two weeks' thirst and hunger tired her
Like a week-old moon hanging wearily

Suddenly she chanced upon a pond
And thought it best to take a bath

She took a dip to cleanse her body
Like a houri in a stream of paradise

~

Khusrau and Shīrīn see each other from a distance but
fail to meet instantly. Overcoming many obstacles,
they finally see each other.

Meanwhile, Khusrau set off on his errand
Hunting beasts on his way for the indigent

At a distance a houri caught his eye
As if a fairy spilling Zamzam water

Her locks unfurled, perhaps to ensnare lovers
The prince was immediately smitten with desire

Her graceful hand was combing her tresses
A hand that could open the locks of paradise

Her silvery figure was white as camphor
She looked like light thrown upon light

Her immaculate eyes hid behind her tresses
Like the moon sliding behind dark clouds

Her face was like a lotus in a pond
Or like a white rose on an earlobe

Her black hair made hyacinths heartsick
Two braids were like two fragrant climbers

Khusrau wondered if she was a fairy
If not a fairy, then a sorcerer's magic

'Her features match with those of Shīrīn
She has cast a spell on me, I am fettered

Oh, how I desire this houri to be Shīrīn!
For she alone can cleanse my heart's rust

Would she cast a glance on me?
I would clasp her like a bouquet'

Shīrīn, on the other hand, was lost in him
'When will that youth come to know me?

Though he rides no decked royal steed
His demeanour is doubtlessly of a king

Should I go near, he might know me?
Should I clasp him, he unbosoms himself

Should I touch him? But he is alone
What shall I tell him in this wilderness?

But if this is not him, I will be misjudging
Give myself to a stranger and lose my worth'

She watched him anxiously and at last
She mounted her horse and sped off

Khusrau paused a little then rushed to the spot
Found nobody there and fell down dejected

Love had sneaked secretly into both hearts
Their first encounter left them craving

Fate did not favour the two longing lovers
Brought them close yet threw them apart

By the time Shīrīn reached Madāin
Khusrau was gone, she wailed wildly

'O my God, what have I done?
How have I let my love escape?

My evil fate has undone me, alas!
I almost had him, now he's gone

He for whom I renounced my kith and kin
Has evaded me and left me distraught

He for whom I have put up with taunts
Unrequited love keeps me languishing

Except you, I seek nothing of the High Throne
Why would I dye my feet with henna now?

With you, I am a mistress of the highest rank
Without you, I am a maiden among maidens

Among my maids was one Malik Nāz
She adorned me from dawn to dusk

I gave them a slip and came running to you
But you left me crying, like a sucking child?'

No garden could bring calm to her heart
Alone she wandered into wilderness

She chose an enclosure on a hillock
Grieving and crying for her love lost

Meanwhile Khusrau reached Armān
Hunting animals in several meadows

Shāpur met the prince on his way
Exhausted, he expressed regret

'I have no knowledge of what befell her
Otherwise Khusrau would not be here'

Khusrau was taken aback and felt depressed
'To whom shall I unburden my heart?

I had her so near and yet did not know
How treacherous is the trick of fate?

Now she is all alone in wilderness
She has neither Shāpur nor Shabdīz

Come, Shāpur, tell me what to do
I shall die if she doesn't come

Perhaps she has taken to mourning
Poor, helpless and grief-stricken

Now rise, gather courage and move
Find her fast and make good the loss'

As Shāpur tracked her into that chamber
He found her broken, nearing death

Shīrīn confronted Shāpur fearlessly
'You, Shāpur, have put me to shame

You know what I have left behind me
I preferred a prison-house to my mansion'

Shāpur said: 'I am not to blame
I was fated for you and Khusrau

Now he has sent me to take you to him
Only a physician can read a sick man's pulse'

Overjoyed, she saddled Shabdīz and galloped away
In the wink of an eye, she reached her lover Khusrau

~

The lovers meet. Shīrīn's mother warns her to be careful
with Khusrau known for his rakishness. Khusrau is
deeply upset at her refusal to give in to his desire.

Face to face, their joy knew no bounds
At last, they were free of grief and pain

Intoxicated with love, desire and passion
Hand in hand, they roamed the meadows

Together they went on hunting expeditions
Walked through thickets of roses and hyacinths

Now Khusrau takes a cup
'Here my love, have a sip'

Drunk, they would fall in each other's arms
Kiss and hold each other in embrace

Now Shīrīn looks askance at Khusrau
'O vintner, you have snatched a kiss from my lips.'

Now Khusrau is annoyed with Shīrīn
'How much will I have to beg for a kiss?'

Now Shīrīn gets a chance to retort
'You have made my crimson cheeks pallid'

Myriad were their ways of love
Refreshing their souls every hour

Shīrīn's companions were alarmed at this
They knew that Khusrau was a reckless man

They asked Mihīn Bānu to warn her:
'Exercise restraint, let not the reins fall off

Khusrau is known for his rakishness
The Prince only looks effeminate

A beautiful girl near an effeminate man
Thinks herself safe and flings caution away

Don't pursue men like the notorious Zulaykha[128]
Be patient in love like the famous Azra[129]

You fell for him and disgraced your kin
Soon he will taunt you for your looseness

You are Shīrīn, frail and tender
He is a lion out on a prowl

You are a delicate rose, he a lustful bulbul
He will have his fun and sully your name

Wine keeps him ever intoxicated
I warn you, guard your chastity

Listen to my sincere, motherly advice
Make him keep his lust under check'

This admonishment made her very upset
She cursed her fate for the turn of events

She reached Khusrau with a heavy heart
He was already infuriated with impatience

Drunk, he tightened his grip around her
And tore the necklace of the anguished girl

'You have oppressed me in devious ways
Tell me, what riches do you want?

Not for a moment can I bear your separation
Desire is burning me, don't ignite it further

Only union's shower can douse this fire
Say yes to my passion without hesitation

You are Shīrīn, the sweet one, sweeten me
Stop being rude and show some mercy

Look around, is there a creature without a pair?
Angels are without pairs, hence nowhere around

Love's rage tames all creatures
No one can resist its mighty grip

What will happen if fire meets gunpowder?
If the beloved lacks mercy, the lover is undone

The rose, the bulbul, the wine server and song
All are here, yet what a pity if there is no union!

It's the hour of leisure, make the best of it
Let us exchange love when we are alone

I plead with you, regard me with kindness
You still have time, tomorrow could be late

I will seek permission from those you fear[130]
Or take you away to any place you want

Or is there someone else in your heart?
Have you given your love to a stranger?'

Deeply shocked, Shīrīn fell into a swoon
Her delicate feelings were much bruised

She grieved for long and cried alone
'How could Khusrau be so stone-hearted?

God knows I have none in my heart but him
Only I guard my chastity with utmost care'

With an ingenious ploy she saved herself
And evaded Khusrau burning with desire

How much she needed Khusrau by her side!
And how he demanded a fee for that!

She kept him in good humour by her cajoling
'I am your maid, you are my Jamshīd and Darius

You have caged me with a bewitching smile
You are the midday sun, I, a midday lamp[131]

I am a humble maid in your service
You have a noble heart, take pity on me

I am yet to taste a wine headier than you
Do I deserve such harshness from you?

You are my wealth, my profit and all
You are the key to my treasure trove

I am an offering lying at your door
Yours is the dagger, kill me or spare me

Let our two clans approve of our match
Otherwise, my name will be sullied forever

Even if you sell me on the slave market
Gladly will I accede to your command'

Khusrau could hardly be cajoled by words
He begged for her favour again and again

'You have driven me crazy for so long
My fairy! What makes you mistrust me?

I promise never to be cross with you
Don't frown on me, talk love to me

Your love has deranged my mind
I am a man weary and forlorn

Love's wound goes deep into my heart
I offer you my life, don't let me down'

~

Shīrīn thinks Khusrau is only flirting with her. Khusrau feels dejected and leaves for Rome where he meets Maryam. Farhād, a young stonecutter, enters the story and falls miserably in love with Shīrīn. Khusrau is alarmed at this and summons him. Failing to dissuade him from harbouring Shīrīn's love, Khusrau promises to give up on her if he cuts through Mount Bīsutun.

He lost all hope of winning Shīrīn's love
And gave up on her with a heavy heart

'She can't fathom the distress of my heart'
He set off to Rome feeling jilted and scorned

The Roman king had a daughter, Maryam
No less than Shīrīn in beauty and charms

How charming and sweet were her ways!
The Prince gladly acknowledged her favours

As Khusrau entered her closet chamber
He enjoyed the delicacy on the offer

Without a drink he forgot Shīrīn
Without venting it his grief vanished

He took Maryam along to Madāin
And began his rule in full majesty

The news put Shīrīn on a thousand thorns
Anguished in soul, she wept day and night

'My friends, well-wishers and maids
Alas, I have lost the apple of my eyes!

Alas, he had begged a favour of me!
But I rebuffed him and he fled away!

I was slow to reckon with his desire
And even slower to sense his aversion

Alas, I could not keep his heart for long!
Alas, I declined to do his bidding!

Before I could see, he went far away
I don't blame him but my grim fate

I let go my game caught in the snare
Pearls collected are now scattered

The rival in love can turn gold to dust
Casting spells, she can rend lovers apart

My rival in love has changed my gold to brass
Her envy makes me a beggar by the door

I don't remember to have taunted anyone
Why has then my spring become winter?

His garden of love I decked with flowers
But the wasp has destroyed the narcissus

I will face disgrace everywhere I go
The cruel one has acted most atrociously

If I will call him, will he pay heed?
Will he remember his frenzied lover?

He has stolen my heart and laid me waste
I would rather die than be unfaithful to him'

Her maids said, 'Gold has value under your ear
A thief always lurks to snatch an object dear

Patience, not grumbling, is love's cure
No doctor can heal its excruciating pain'

She made a resolve, called her maids
And reached Madāin to claim her love

Instantly, the news reached Khusrau
'Shīrīn is looking madly for you'

He ran to Maryam's chamber
Seeking solace and her advice

'I hear Shīrīn is back to claim me
Counsel me, how to deal with her

I swear by you I have made a resolve
Not to take her as long as I have you

Still, could I ask you to put up with her?
Or keep her as a maid, one among many?'

No sooner had Khusrau uttered these words
Than Maryam was beyond herself with rage

'Renounce her now or I call my father
The army of Rome will obliterate you

Can you suffer an arrow shot in your eyes?
Can your body suffer being burnt alive?'

Khusrau sent for the trusted Shāpur
'Come, Shāpur, you have a task at hand?

Go, tell Shīrīn she need not grieve
Maryam is not the woman I want

My love for Shīrīn is deep as the sea
Soon I will go to meet her myself

If she agrees, bring her with you
Let her bless me with her presence

She is wise and knows my state well
She is at liberty to choose her stay'

Shāpur carried Khusrau's missive to Shīrīn
She fell like a tree axed by a woodcutter

'Shāpur, I can't go to him from here
Here I shall wait for him to come

If he deems fit, let him visit me here
Or else send me a lock of his hair

The meaning of his message I can intuit
He waters my leaves, axes my roots

Though Mihīn Bānu's death was a blow to me
I followed her advice and ruined my life

The past is past, let us start afresh
I am too naive, lead me to light

In the world of toils and misery
I am ablaze with the love of Parvaiz[132]

Sinners will have their place in hell there
Away from him I am burning here

Listen, my sole sustenance is sweet milk
But I get it late in the afternoon

Can you find me a skilful craftsman?'
So, the zestful Farhād was called

Shīrīn addressed him with respect
'May you prosper by day and night!'

She observed his tall stature
And summoned him for a word

She pleaded with him in earnest
'I need to have milk each day

Bring out a milk canal from this mount
I promise we shall be friends ever after'

Farhād was much taken by her beauty
Tears of love flowed from his two springs

Senses benumbed, he fell on his knees
His world had turned upside down

Very kindly Shīrīn helped him to his feet
'You are known for your strength, do not act so'

He got down to work and dug out a stream
From her resplendent face he drew strength

In no time people carried this news to Khusrau
'Farhād, a young man, has a crush on Shīrīn

The stone cutter has performed an amazing feat
He has pierced the heart of a rocky mountain

And brought forth a milk stream by his craft
Now he feasts his eyes on her pretty face

Poison from her hand is sweet to him
He serves her like a faithful slave

His utter devotion to her is stunning
He is an angel in the human guise

Alone in woods he sings her praise
And composes love poems for her

Shīrīn too holds him in high esteem
Farhād has made a place in her soul'

Envy stung Khusrau, he lay his crown aside
Farhād was summoned without losing time

Farhād stood head high in the royal presence
His towering stature impressed the king

'What's your name?' Khusrau asked
'Names have no value,' he replied

'Do you have parents?' Khusrau asked
'All I have is before you,' he replied

'Where do you come from?' Khusrau inquired
'I belong to no place,' came the curt answer

'What do you desire?' Khusrau asked
'Majnun wants Layla, no less, no more'

'What will you take to give up on her?'
'Offer me the whole world, it is futile'

'So, it is Shīrīn that you want!'
'A blind man wants two seeing eyes'

'Stop speaking in riddles, who are you?'
'A mountain-cutter and her lover'

'Erase her from your heart,' thundered Khusrau
'Only when my eyes turn blind,' said Farhād

'You don't deserve her,' taunted Khusrau
'You are so wrong, measure up yourself'

'Forget Shīrīn!' Khusrau threatened
'Don't give yourself airs,' said Farhād

Khusrau continued, 'Do you have any worries?'
'None whatsoever except that of Shīrīn'

Khusrau roared, 'By God, I will slay you'
Farhād shot back, 'My head is on offer'

This exchange continued for some time
Until Khusrau was fed up and let him go

Confounded, he addressed his courtiers
'Never have I heard such witty retorts

My wise ministers, find some way out
He is about to take away my Shīrīn'

They deliberated and hit upon an idea
Farhād had to be got by a wily trick

He was summoned and offered a deal
'Go, make a path through Mount Bīsutun'

'We promise you Shīrīn if you succeed
She will be your reward when you are done'

The elated Farhād accepted the offer
He took a pickaxe to cleave the rocks

First, he carved her image on a big stone
A beautiful image, a replica of the damsel

The engraver filled the image with colours
And soon its fame spread far and wide

Gazing the image would satiate his hunger
He lost himself to its charm and beauty

He girded up his loins to have his reward
Under his feet the solid rock turned to dust

Though constant hewing chafed his hands
Sweet thoughts of Shīrīn eased his burden

'God, can I pull through the two travails[133]
To you alone, I complain of grim my fate

Will my wailing calls reach her ears?
Your slave begs you, my merciful God!'

Apparently devoted to an image in stone
In truth he mellowed into a selfless man

'Cutting through the rocks, my eyes are worn
And I have little hope of seeing her again

I have turned the course of mountain streams
And braved the mortal threats of Khusrau

I waste away for a love that sleeps
In vain I keep watching for her

Ah, such callous disregard of the sweetheart!
And such forbidding toughness of the rocks!'

At last, his sincere prayers were answered
And Shīrīn's heart inclined to see him

His wails forced an answer from God
His heart's wish came to fruition

Shīrīn was enjoying her friends' company
Seated in ease, busy in laughter and gaiety

Suddenly she remembered Farhād
'I must see how he is doing,' she thought

She set out to have a look herself
Alone she rode into the mountains

She saw her portrait engraved in the stone
Tied her horse Shabrang and went ahead

She found him grovelling in the dust
Days of crushing toil had taken their toll

She picked him up softly like a rose
He saw her and gave out a loud cry

She said:
'My head I offer you, let me kiss your feet
Caress your bruised hands with my own

Have you borne such disgrace for my sake?
Till Judgement Day I am yours from now

You were destined to see this for my sake'
She wept bitterly crying out, 'My Farhād!

I am to blame for your woeful state
I am to blame for your abasement

Won't you take a sip from Shīrīn's cup?'
'Your name Shīrīn is enough for me,' he said

She said, 'O wise, sagacious Farhād
Pardon me this passing tribulation'

The steep climb exhausted Shabrang
Shīrīn began to worry for her horse

Suddenly, it stumbled and fell down
Shīrīn was distraught to see it dead

Farhād lifted both her and the horse
And carried them home on his shoulder

Crying, he bid her farewell and returned
She wished him best for the remaining task

That was the last that he saw of her
That was his last day and last night

~

Khusrau resorts to a trick to get rid of Farhād.

It is said that when Khusrau got to know
Farhād's victory over rocks and her heart

He was alarmed and called his advisors
'Tell me how to deal with this menace

I have promised him Shīrīn for this
Alas, I have put my life on a wager!

If he takes her, I shall surely die
My life stays or departs with her'

They said, 'Only one way remains
Let's announce Shīrīn's death'

An old wise woman was fetched
Bent with age like a crooked bow

She was dispatched to Mount Bīsutun
As she reached there, she gave a cry

'Come, luckless Farhād, hear this news
Your love Shīrīn is dead, go to her place'

'How can that be?' he screamed
'Whom can I send there to see?

Gone are the youthful days of promise
I collected water from rocks, now it's drained

The royal falcon has flown far away
Who is that who grudged me my love?'

Crying, he embraced Shīrīn's portrait
Ripping apart his own soul in grief

He took his axe and struck himself dead
'Come, Farhād, lie down with Shīrīn'

The news reached Khusrau and Shīrīn
She was overcome with immense grief

She rode to the rugged mountains
Shedding tears of grief on the way

She called out to Farhād in the rocks
And found him dead at a distance

Like a tall cypress's shadow fallen supine
A rose in his hair, face smeared with dust

She took him in her lap howling in pain
And cleansed his dusty feet with her hair

'Wake up, Farhād, my friend, do tell me
Who has spilled your innocent blood?

Wake up Farhād, did you ask for a drink?
And now you have drained the cup of grief

Wake up Farhād, rise to your feet
See how your pain makes me groan

Wake up Farhād, this separation is fatal
My nights and days are an endless pain

O Farhād, what a simpleton have you been!
Your enemies tricked you with a false word

Wake up Farhād, I give you my promise
I am yours till the Judgement, please wait

I hail your purity a hundred times
You rank high among pure lovers'

Come, Mahmud Gāmi, be brief
Consider the lot of the lovers now

~

Shīrīn mourns Farhād's death. Khusrau sends her a letter taunting her.

It is said after Farhād was dead
Shīrīn mourned for a long time

Afflicted, aggrieved, she bore with her lot
Maids and servants would lull her to sleep

Farhād was shrouded in linen and buried
Shīrīn spent a treasure in his name

Built a shrine for him, a symbol of love
A pavilion furnished with gorgeous carpets

Spies carried all this to King Khusrau
'The hapless lover has suffered greatly

Deprived of both his life and Shīrīn
He died craving for his sweetheart'

The news of Shīrīn ruffled Khusrau
He shot a letter of condolence to her

'Farhād, the mighty man died young
Death is inevitable, his time had come

Apparently, he is mingled with dust
In truth he lives as a selfless lover

He was your true friend and comforter
Smitten by an enticing glance from you

A gutsy lover fully devoted to you
You carry the burden of his death

A glance from you pierced through him
He lost his senses and died haplessly

Love's affliction struck him hard
A flicker of your eyes smote him dead

If you are grieving, I too am sad
God knows how you might kill me!

His love drove you to the mountains
With a single maid you rushed to him

I came to you begging for a glimpse
O rude love, you scorned me callously

You ruined the poor man's life
Why do you pretend melting like an icicle now?

Why value people after they are dead?
Forget the dead, be good to the living

You beguiled him by a deceptive glance
Your pretence of love killed the lover

In truth, he died by your arrow
How many more will you kill?

You are a lightning bolt from the sky
Devotion to you is a treacherous trap

You are responsible for his death
But let that pass, think of the future

Killing an innocent man in this life is
A burden you bear till the Judgement

Dressed in black, you are mourning his death
Farhād is gone and will never come back

Your delicate body will wear out fast
And your cheeks' redness will fade away

Your figure will start quaking with age
And your kindred spirit will desert you[134]

Seize the moment, forget this mourning
Youth is a blessing, don't fritter it away

Heed my counsel, I wish you well
Stop the display of endless grieving'

Khusrau's letter left Shīrīn benumbed
Her eyes shed blood, wounds ached anew

'Alas, he taunts me for Farhād's love!
My friend was a victim of his animosity

Once my heart brimmed with Khusrau's love
And I spent my time always pining for him

Deserting me, he took many others
Disgraced me as a prisoner of grief

He was too discourteous to ask after me
And hard-hearted enough not to kill me[135]

Pitying me, God sent me a friend
An angel he was in the human form

How shall I say what the noble soul did?
He dug the earth to draw a stream of milk

They tricked him with a false promise
The pitiless king shunned all goodness

"Go", he was told, "Shīrīn is yours
If only you can cut through the rocks"

Once in the mountains he set to work
Rejoicing in the thoughts of winning me

Khusrau was shamed by my boldness
And had him killed by means of a ruse

In the rocks he carved a path and a stream
His feat has done all humble men proud

I thus cry over my love lost forever
A love who had full claim on me

Though death comes to all high and low
His death has exposed me to a cruel world

Wise men have a pithy saying:
"Don't mock others so that you are not mocked"

While I am mourning, he shows such conceit
Sunlight and shade keep changing their place'[136]

~

Khusrau's wife dies. Now Shīrīn taunts him.

Meanwhile, Khusrau's wife Maryam died
Now it was his turn to sit for mourning

Maryam, the daughter of the king of Rome
Had died too young, she was just fourteen

She had given birth to an ill-starred child
Shuriya was his name, a would-be patricide

Her death left Khusrau broken-hearted
His gaiety turned into bitter sorrow

When Shīrīn came to know of her demise
She wrote a complaint in condolence's guise

'Lord, may the King Khusrau live long!
What if a rose from the garden is gone?

Granted that your devoted Maryam is dead
Out of a thousand maids you have lost one

You still have one less than a thousand left
All beautiful, full-breasted, silvery figures

How was she more special than me?
Why has her death stung you such?

Oh yes, only the sufferer knows sorrow's meaning
But you are a king, mourning ill becomes you

I am an orphan, have no siblings or children
I only had Farhād but you sent him to doom

No sooner do you rejoice in a foe's death
Than you lose a very dear one of yours

Prudence means submission to Fate
No shield can blunt the arrow of Fate'

~

Affronted by Shirin's letter, Khusrau sets off to see
Shakar.

As the King read through the reproof
He bid Shāpur to gird up his loins

'Shīrīn is indeed scorching my soul
I have had enough of her sarcasm

You must rise now and go to Isfahān
A damsel lives there, Shakar is her name

She is lovelier than either Shīrīn or Maryam
And the only medicine for my bitter pain'

Viziers and counsellors warned Khusrau
'She is like the moon shining everywhere[137]

Heed our warning, she's not worthy of you
You will surely realize how wrong you are

If you don't trust us, go, keep an eye on her
Quietly she will sneak into your chamber'

Smitten with desire, Khusrau rode off
Richly dressed in his royal costumes

The same night he reached Isfahān
Searching desperately for her street

Late in the night he sent her a message
She told her maids, 'My lover is here'

She was adorned with pearls and gold
Shakar became a look-alike of Shīrīn

She decked her tresses and came out in pomp
Amidst intoxicating wines, music and festivity

Khusrau melted with passion's heat
He lost his sense and heart's solace

Maidens were standing row upon row
Having Khusrau, Shakar was overjoyed

She took great delight in royal hospitality
Together they retired into the royal mansion

The two lovers shared intimate moments
And soon they were busy in lovemaking

They were merry in each other's embrace
And made the best of their intimacy

The wrestler grappled hard but was floored
Khusrau's desire was too quickly spent

'Shakar' is sold in loads on the market[138]
Flies and ants run to nibble at it

Candy is a delicacy relished by the kings
'Shakar' is meant for the lowly soldiers

Again, Khusrau's mind turned to Shīrīn
'When will her proud heart melt for me?'

He ordered Shāpur to abandon Shīrīn
Alone, she felt more miserable than ever

Khusrau felt helpless and called Shāpur
'My soul is seething with love's fire

Has her stony heart softened a bit?
Has she remembered Khusrau once?

I am her slave; let her treat me as she will
I have risen from the dust under her feet'

～

Meanwhile, Shīrīn gives vent to her feelings.

'If I, your first love, had a place in your heart
Pray, how could you then live without me?

You are a king with a rising fortune
I have lost both my crown and love

You got busy in your kingly affairs
And ditched this miserable soul

Don't humiliate Shīrīn any more
The only lady of the Roman breed

To get Shakar you rode to Isfahān
While I lingered long in wait here

Day and night you have fun with maids
While I burn and melt like a candle

Your actions have sullied my good name
Shame has eaten into my flesh and bones'

Khusrau retorted, 'I am reduced to dust
It's not you but I who is sorrow-wrecked

To all appearance I have been a king
But without you no more than a beggar'

Shīrīn heard him and spoke boldly
First knitting her brows into a frown

'Why do you keep shirking away?
Your love has scorched my each fibre

Trusting my destiny, I divorced my kin
But did not foresee a false lover

Love's arrow has gone through me
I, Shīrīn, harbour many cravings

Though love's load pulls down my heart
The strength of my nerves suffices me

Your wealth and pomp mean nothing to me
Your bragging of love is an empty talk'

Despaired of her, Khusrau left dejected
Shīrīn's bitter words had jilted him

He lost all hope of winning her love
Looking back wistfully he walked off

With a heavy heart and tearful eyes
Khusrau returned to his entourage

As the night fell, he called Shāpur
And related to him his doleful tale

'With high hopes I had gone to her
I found her haughty and unrelenting

I pleaded with her in every way
She was dry and prickly as a thorn

Don't ask how I beseeched her indulgence
Invoking many pious names to coax her

Once, her company used to rejoice me
Now she has turned cold, merciless

Like a beggar, she made me wait outside
I spent my night in pitch darkness

You know well what all I did for her
And how badly I wished she were here

Never again will I knock her door
No good will come to me from her'

Shāpur heard this, then said, 'O King
Her heart is burnt and her soul weary

In your pursuit she has borne disgrace
Pardon me, you have done little for her

Surely her heart is suffused with your love
You are her crown that she proudly wears

Utter devotion is the first condition of love
Next you must bear with the beloved's apathy

Good time has come, be free of care
No less is a woman's love for a man

Were she to shut herself behind a door
She'll grow restless and crave for her partner

Cheer up, keep your heart from running berserk
Show patience, Shīrīn will surely come to you'

That very moment Khusrau fell asleep
Pure red wine had soothed his senses

~

Shīrīn misses Khusrau badly.

It is said when Khusrau had left Shīrīn
Her entire world had turned upside down

She had beaten her head against rocks
And battered her stony heart with stones

Lost all patience, sense and strength
And rushed out alone looking for him

Now she ran after Khusrau crying aloud
And reached his tent that very night

The tent was resonant with lovely music
That very moment Shāpur stepped out of it

~

*Shīrīn and Khusrau exchange a few words. She retires
as Khusrau refuses to see her point. She prays for a
change of his heart. Her prayers are answered and
Khusrau yields before her firmness.*

'What if I am in exile now?
I still can look after myself

What if I have given you my heart?
Still no one can instil fear in me

What if joy came my way and went?
Still my youth has not worn away

What if grief has bent me like a weeping willow?
I can still make the sun crazy

What if I pursued you like a slave girl?
My pearl has not seen a diamond yet'[139]

The king said, 'You did not accede to my wish
Pining for the rose, a sad heart was crushed

Beauty, don't be proud, leave bashfulness
Grant me that which I desire of you'

She said, 'Dodging the issue serves no end
One need not test the tested again

You have battered my sweet delicate soul
And wounded my stout heart with spears

Leading your men, you are on an errand
You only pretend to be waiting for me

You have ever been haughty and reckless
Ruthless, inconsiderate and blazing like fire

Once more you might indulge me
But, alas, old habits die very hard!'

Khusrau said:
'Why is my delicacy still unripe?
And union with you still far away?

You wasted many days and nights on me
Enough now, I have been requited for that

My kind-hearted love, I have suffered much
To see you again was my heart's great desire

Be pleased or annoyed, the choice is yours
But if you don't relent, I will torch myself'

Shīrīn replied:
'Listen, O King, I will mince no words
Never will I let go the hold of virtue'

Her words made Khusrau unhappy
His heart was branded like a tulip

He said, 'O coquettish love *sans* mercy
Speaking daggers is not new to you

I have nursed great affection for you
Lost my days' rest and nights' sleep

You jilted me and went after Farhād
He waited in vain, your affection vanished

Poor man, how great was his suffering!
He lived in mountains and hewed rocks

Like a daytime robber you ravaged his heart
Your laughter lit a fire and burnt him up'

She said, 'Do you forget the Great Reckoning?
Mock me for Farhād's love, how evil of you?

Though he struck himself dead for me
To me he was like a long-lost brother[140]

A peerless craftsman of numerous arts
Whose blood is a burden on your head

Now my being is wrecked by grief
Black disgrace has fallen to my lot

To show me down was your real design
To set me afire your heart's true wish'

Shīrīn retired crying floods of tears
Crazed by the sting of love's sorrow

'My God, no one comforts me
Have pity on me, hear my wails!

I am helpless, infirm and forsaken
Disgraced, abused and powerless

Away from home, wandering in exile
At the mercy of my heartless foes

Protect my honour with your grace
Secure the veil of my chastity

Like a candle I keep burning and melting
My days are restless, my nights sleepless

He is proud, unruly and loveless
I have wasted my youth after him

My childhood was spent in innocent pleasures
Love, however, is an overwhelming force'

Her tears forced an answer from Heaven
Khusrau arrived with the dawn's break

Shīrīn sensed the coming of joy
And got ready for the occasion

She closed the doors and went to the attic
Anticipating his arrival, she made preparations

Khusrau arrived at the closed door
He thought he was scorned again

He called a maid to know the truth
'Tell me, how does your lady fare?

What stone has she found in my heart?
Why has the door been closed on me?

Go inside and give her my greetings
Her slave, not a king, seeks permission

A poor man has left his home for her
Ask her if he should stay or leave

My love for her surpasses hers for me
I can prove that if she opens the door

I have come with high hopes
My love for her is boundless'

The maid took his message to Shīrīn
A soul sunk in sorrow was cheered up

'Go back to Khusrau,' she ordered
'Make sure he is not sad or annoyed'

The maid followed her lady's instructions
Told Khusrau all she was asked to

He waxed eloquent in apologizing
Overwhelming her with his humility

A six-stepped pavilion was raised instantly
The lovers eyed each other from afar

Hands folded, Khusrau stood before her
'Your black tresses have wrecked my heart

Pardon me my long absence from you
Now let us think of the future course'

Shīrīn did not mince her words
'Surely, you are not flirting again?

A reformed man I cannot spurn
But I can't be had without a dower'

A marvellous couch on a golden carpet
Khusrau and Shīrīn sat face to face

Then Khusrau went around spreading the word
He announced his wedding in his kingdom

Kings were invited from far and wide
The rich and the poor thronged to the feast

King Khusrau stood out among all of them
Exquisitely dressed in his splendid attire

Slaves, maidens, graceful attendants
Old friends and new, all had assembled

Khusrau enjoyed the moment of union
All were gay, save the luckless Farhād

Delightful music filled the air
Khusrau took Shīrīn inside

She was escorted into a fabulous room
Furnished with velvet, brocade and silk

The golden carpets were most wondrous
The bride and the groom reclined at ease

Her tresses hung down to the hems
Like black slaves with shining bodies

Her dark enticing eyes enchanted all
And wine sharpened her coquetry

Her arched brows shot amorous darts
Bringing down mendicants and hermits

Fatal arrows flying from her sharp eyelashes
Pierced through the defences of many a man

Two hyacinths hanging by the rose
Perplexed the bulbuls' quivering hearts

The mole on her cheek marvelled at itself
Like an enemy's heart burning in envy's fire

Each strand of her hair was braided
Fawns lay ensnared in her eyebrows

Her eardrops looked like dancing white lilies
Their dangling robbed even the shrewd hearts

Her neck more lustrous than a shining medal
Comparable only to the groom's pearl necklace

He gazed on her bosom whiter than the snow
Brighter than a mirror and clearer than a crystal

Two glowing silvery embers within her flanks
Like two pomegranates craved by ailing men[141]

A comfort for bodies, a solace for souls
Her hair-thin waist lay hid inside her robe

When she smiled she scattered candy
And Khusrau's heart bloomed like a rose

'Behold the garden of my beauty,' she said
'Let's celebrate union among blooming tulips'

Passion drove them in each other's embrace
He removed the lid from the delicacy's dish

He gazed the thornless bud in the garden
No serpent guarded the hidden treasure

On a silvery bed the two became one
The pearl was pierced, love consummated

Drunk with wine, they heaved with passion
And lay together on a brocade couch

The bodies of two lovers were joined
The two passionate bosoms clung tight

The warmth of her breasts refreshed his heart
How pleasant is such warmth on a cold night!

Shīrīn's lips sought out those of Khusrau
His heart drowned in the well of her chin

Lips were fixed to lips, cheek pressed against cheek
And the two faces wrapped by dark tresses

The union endeared them to each other
For a long time the two lay like this

Let the veil fall on the lovers' meet
Suffice it to say the two became one

~

Khusrau becomes a victim of patricide. Shīrīn kills herself.

Now, Shuriya was Khusrau's only son
An impious child who rebelled against him

His lustful eyes were set on Shīrīn
He imprisoned both her and the king

One evening he summoned all servants
And ordered them to disperse quickly

As the night fell the depraved usurper
Sneaked out with a dagger in hand

He found Khusrau and Shīrīn asleep
Heavy with the wine they had drunk

He plunged the dagger into his father
Blood spurted from his wounded heart

Khusrau awoke to see the wicked son
Half dead, he asked for a sip of water

'Shīrīn is in a sweet slumber,' he thought
'She should not witness this gory scene

She's my worry, I care least for myself
What if she wakes from her sleep?

Come, O self, you have to die one day!
And bear the pain of parting till the Judgement

When she sees me dead, she'll kill herself
But I can't muster courage to do the act'

Alas, Khusrau was dead before long!
Shīrīn felt the of warmth of his blood

She awoke and saw him drenched in blood
A lifeless figure staring with his ossified eyes

She wailed and shed pearl-like tears
'This indeed is Shuriya's doing

O my tulip-cheeked love, let me rock you in my lap
If you feel drowsy, you'll sleep in my heart

Open your almond-like eyes and look at me
Where have you gone, darkening my days?

Loved by you, I was a blooming daffodil
Cut off from you, I am now withered

For whom should I now adorn myself?
I am driven mad, where can I see you?

Without you, life is too big a burden
Without you, no place is fit for me'

Dawn broke and the sun rose high
She cleaned his stains with her hair

She washed his body with camphor water
And shrouded him in bright white linen

All her wealth she gave away as charity
Gold, jewels, pearls, all in his name

Then she circled around Khusrau's body
Burning like a moth in the flame of love

Showering pearls she carried him in a bier
Put him in his grave and lay by his side

She took a dagger and drove it in her chest
And clasped Khusrau tightly to herself

All who saw this broke into lamentation
Nothing but disgrace fell to Shuriya's lot

Shīrīn, Farhād, Khusrau all are dead
But the tale of the lovers will never die

Come, O Mahmud Gāmi, end this tale
And look once more to the lovers' state

Countless blessings of God be on Nizāmi
A servant at his door is Mahmud Gāmi

~

O Mahmud Gāmi, you are indeed Jāmi
Or let us call you Kashmir's Nizāmi

By the order of Shah Habibullah Malik[142]
I have finished writing this poem

On a Wednesday in the month of *Safar*[143]
I have rendered the poem in Kashmiri

The year is Eleven Hundred and Ninety-nine
By the reckoning of the Hijrah calendar[144]

Hail Shīrīn for her majestic death!
And hail her giving and taking life![145]

This is the way one should die in love
And surrender one's life to the Creator

Let him be engulfed by God's blessings
Who warmly remembers the writer here!

2. Yusuf Zulaykha

Zulaykha, a princess, has three consecutive dreams in which she sees a very handsome young man, is smitten with him, and thinking him to be a nobleman of Egypt, sends him a proposal. After the wedding, she realizes that she has married a wrong man. A heavenly voice assures her that she will find the man of her dreams.

Let every page begin with God's infinite praise
Followed by blessings on the holy Prophet

Stay with me for a while and listen to this tale
Love's ardour I relate for those who would care

Far off in a Western land there lived a king, Taimus
His daughter's peerless beauty had become famous

Zulaykha, a heart-ravisher, as luminous as the full moon
Crystal-bosomed, whose body put all mirrors to shame

Of her many gifts was a pair of silvery dome-like breasts
A mere look at which turned many hearts upside down

Her mole and graceful forelocks scattered on her face
The eyes of her ringlets ambushed many a wayfarer

No one else in the land could match her beauty
At a very tender age she felt a fervid surge of love

A charming handsome youth appeared to her in a
dream
Of immense beauty, scented tresses and a moon-like
brow

His curled locks were lassoes that he threw all around
His mole was a rue seed, burning in the midst of fire

His stately stature raised commotion of a hundred
doomsdays
Ah, his silvery face, scented locks, fragrant body, fiery
looks!

Cypress-statured, his gazelle eyes looked sharply
around
A moon-like heart-ravisher who put lions to flight

Zulaykha witnessed the young man in full splendour
His arched eyebrows, his eyelashes sharp as arrows

His pearl-scattering mouth, his dagger-like nose
All these and more she saw and lost her repose

A second time that youth of devastating beauty
showed
His intoxicating cheeks and limbs bright as the moon

When he appeared a third time, she asked his name and place
'I belong to Egypt and am a noble in the royal court'[146]

She woke crying, 'God, where has the moon's face hidden?'
Out of wits, she ran everywhere to catch a glimpse of his

She wept, 'Where's he gone with my heart and senses?
Wretched I am, to whom shall I complain of my agony?'

She cried, tore her garment and smeared herself with dust
'You will scorch me, wear me out, and expose me to taunts'

Maids gathered around her, 'You've wilted like a jasmine'
Comforting and caressing her, they asked her the secret

'A winsome face has showed up and left me desolate
A visage exuding divine light, a lord of beauty's empire

A thousand moths keep circling his candle-like face
They burn and bleed, but he's too absorbed in himself

As the night fell, my eyes caught his black snake-like
lock
Tyrannous and elusive, he has stolen my sick heart

He is Egypt's high noble, I, a lowly maid to him
Ah, for the day I shall have him face to face!'

Her father heard the clamour and felt aggrieved
'My strength is sapped by your act, my dear daughter

That man is no match to us,' he admonished her
'Your obsession will shame me and soil my good name

You are a genuine pearl, he only a counterfeit one
Brass sorts badly with gold, friend and foe will mock me

How many princes of high birth yearn to have you!
Choose any one of them whose looks you fancy'

'I'm tied to that noble, I don't want anyone else
I am pleased with Fate's decree that stupefies sense

When two lovers strike a chord, let the whole world
grumble
In Heaven's eyes, jasper may fetch more than a pearl.'

Taimus relented and offered Zulaykha to the noble
Who accepted the proposal with his soul and heart

Loads of rich gifts from him reached Zulaykha's
house
Her wish had come true, her joy knew no bounds

With all blandishments she set off joyfully for Egypt
With rich gifts the noble came out to welcome her

His very mention filled her heart with great delight
'My grief is gone today, I have a reason to rejoice'

As she sneaked through the screen to catch his
glimpse
Her wits flew away, she dropped like a wilted rose

She shrieked, 'Where's he who plundered my soul?
Where's he who drove me from home to languish
here?

Not he who beguiled me in my dream
Not he who burnt me like a dry twig

Not he whose glimpse threw me into the tempest
And lured me to get stuck in Egypt's sandbank

Not he whose snake-like tresses have stung me
Not he whose passion has set my soul ablaze

Certainly not the man who made me desert my parents
My grief is unspeakable; a little girl has lost her earring!

I am duped and waylaid, pray, whose prize am I now?
O love's monstrous fate, where shall I find him now?'

Suddenly, a heavenly voice comforted her heart:
'We will keep you chaste and lead you to your lover'

Her hopes hanging in balance, she reached the noble
Withered, scorched and shedding pearl-like tears

Yoked now, she would sneak out into the open
Roam about in the streets looking for her love

She sighed and wept but found no clue of her love
'I ache for the one who has denied himself to me!'

Mahmud, look how love's agony gnaws at lovers
They live a living death, their tales only endure

~

A Song of Separation

'I am waiting for you to come
When will you show up?

Speech fails this hapless Zulaykha
Now an exile in Egypt
You belong here, yet hide yourself
When will you show up?

O rose without the bulbul!
Which garden have you bloomed in?
If you heed, I will tell you
my sorry tale

You are winsome and alluring
And your absence is fatal
Wake up, my love deep in slumber!
O archer riding the steed!
You have shot a fatal arrow
My heart you have ripped to shreds
With brows bent like bows
O commander victorious!

You have stung me, O viper!
My eyes have dimmed now
Love's sickness can kill me
Come, I will carve you a bed of sandalwood
And offer you my heart and soul
My heart is no more a single piece!

O my youth's bloom, my pearl necklace!
My summer has turned to autumn
My youthful days are rolling fast
In vain I weep copious tears
You have burnt my soul
O my soulmate of childhood!

Come to me, my tormentor
Let your maid have a glimpse of you
O sorcerer with black eyes!

My fragile heart is shattered
Defenceless against the pain of parting
O rose,
O my red pomegranate flower
When will you turn up?

I have no clue of where you are
I am axed, I wander bewildered
O world, wily and treacherous!
What is that you want of me?

Could I buy you for the whole world?
O necklace of my bosom
My golden earring!147

And if you desert me
I am not worth a farthing

I, friendless, helpless Zulaykha
am worthless without you
You might have torched many more
in love's vaulting flame
But none as much as I!'

Mahmud keeps trilling his song
When will you turn up?

~

Yusuf's childhood.

Yusuf was Yaqub's dearest son[148]
His radiant face lit up the world

The moon of Canaan was a king of beauties[149]
A calamity for hearts, a plunderer of souls

His ruddy cheeks had a moon-like lustre
He titillated hearts with his sprightly gait

Long-necked, as lithe as a cypress
Tossing his serpentine tresses around

Curls clustered around his lovely face
Like a black viper on a rosebush

His dishevelled tresses were snares of love
A calamity for faith and piety

The black mole was a negro boy
Seated on display at the port of Surat[150]

The mole enmeshed by the curly locks
A fawn entangled in a hunter's net

His hair flowed straight like hyacinths
Tumbling down from top to toe

His black almond eyes gave a kingly look
A shining pearl necklace lit up his cheeks

A coquette with a brow like the Turkish bow
Sharp eyelashes grew on his gazelle eyes

His beaming chin was an unsettling sight
Lovers often found their hearts quiver

His waist was finer than a strand of hair
Mouth like a bud, tongue sweet as sugar

He had lips rosier than a red ruby
No diamond could have paid their price

A polished youth with pearl-like teeth
Glistening behind the screening veil

His charms were drops of quicksilver
A quick remedy for the ailing hearts

He had lost his mother as a child
And was brought up by his aunt

Yaqub lavished great affection on him
Was mindful of him day and night

He used to bow to his arched brows
And often kiss his jasmine cheeks

With hands and feet dyed in henna
The boy used to sleep beside his father

While asleep he would shine
Like the moon in a limpid pool

One night he woke with a start
A strange dream had shaken him

Yaqub said, 'Tell me what you saw'
'Be calm, father, I will speak soon

The sun, the moon and eleven stars
I saw fallen prostrate before me'

'Don't share it with your half-brothers
Or else they will snatch you from me.'

But the brothers learnt the secret
Envy robbed them of sleep and rest

They made plans to destroy him
'Our father has no affection for us'[151]

They came to their father together
Bowed to him and said in one voice:

'Father, Yusuf is lonely and distressed
Why don't you send him with us?

He will roam about hills and meadows
And make wreaths of meadow flowers

From ewe's milk, butter and cheese
He will make sweets all day'

'No way can I send him with you!
I can't have him away from me

Lest he should fall asleep somewhere
And a prowling wolf carry him away'

'These fears are ill-founded, Father
There are eleven of us, all sturdy'

Yaqub gave in under their pleading
But deep inside he had a foreboding

They lured Yusuf into wilderness
Threw him down and thrashed him

His was beaten black and blue
His lotus body was discoloured

He asked his brothers entreatingly
'Why are you thrashing an innocent child?

O brothers, my dear ones, desist
O God, my dear God, rescue me!

Barefoot, I stand on piercing thorns
God, you are a witness to my state!

Brothers, don't handle me so roughly
Show some mercy, let me walk softly

Where do you want to kill me?
God, you know I am alone!'

He cried out in great anguish
Like a fawn writhing in a trap

They threw him into a deep well
Just then Jibrīl descended from Heaven[152]

'Don't grieve, you are a chosen prophet
You will be rescued after three days

Donned in the raiment of Khalīl[153]
Or one sent by God Himself'

Jibrīl untied a talisman he wore
And wound it around his body

In the middle there was a stone
Like Nooh's ark in the great deluge[154]

Slowly Yusuf seated himself on the stone
And his presence turned the water sweet

Every day the brothers came to mock him
'How do you fare in the bottom of the well?

How do you spend your time there?
Do you still give thanks to the Almighty?'

On the third day some merchants arrived
Searching for water they came to the well

They lowered a pail down to its bottom
And Yusuf came out like a shining sun

His face threw a flood of radiance around
They hid him from every ear and eye

'How beautiful is this boy!
He is peerless in all respects'

When the brothers came to see Yusuf
They could not find him in the well

In fury they rushed to the merchants
'Bring forth our slave you have stolen

A lousy boy who did nothing but sleep
We threw him in the well as a reprimand

You can have him for a price
Else he goes back into the well'

Yusuf was thus sold to the merchants
For a sum too paltry to mention

The uncouth sellers were themselves duped
They had traded saffron for a bunch of leeks

Bartering pure gold for base brass
They signed the transaction deal

The merchants were happy with their bargain
They had a jewel for just a few pennies

Having sold him, brothers returned home
Wailing aloud, 'O our dear brother!'

They reached their father, shedding tears
And showed him Yusuf's bloodstained shirt

Yaqub's bright day turned pitch dark
'I had sensed this on that day,' he said

'My sons, Yusuf's brothers, for God's sake
Tell me what has befallen him'

They came to him dragging a wolf
'He carried off Yusuf,' they said

Yaqub saw the wolf and burst into tears
Trees wept too and stones cracked with pain

'O wolf,' he said, 'why did you do it?
Why did you tear into my dearest son?'

Tears began to flow from the wolf's eyes
Though petrified, he began to speak

'Yaqub', he said, 'I swear by God
I too am sundered from my mate

I have never seen or heard of Yusuf
I hide nothing, say nothing but truth

I wandered all day through pastures and glades
They trapped me wickedly and brought me here'

Truth delivered the guiltless wolf
God united him with his mate

But Yaqub was left wailing
Grief began to eat into him

'My dear son, my Yusuf
Where shall I wait for you?

You left with your half-brothers
But never returned to your father

I caught a whiff of their intentions
I knew they were bent on foul play

I can't bear being away from you
Don't forsake your old father!

My life I will sacrifice for you
Let me have a glimpse of you

I nursed you, rocked you on my knee
Your absence stings me like a viper

This old Yaqub is lying in wait
Asking birds for a clue of yours

O birds, have you chanced on him?
Yusuf, that fawn-eyed darling of mine

When he smiles, it's like a bud sprouting
He looks like a moon rising on the horizon

Son, who slit your soft lofty neck?
Did you scream at that moment?

Did your red cheeks turn black?
Did pity not touch your slayer?

My handsome son, O wondrous darling!
A candle snuffed out, where are you?

Your absence is a crushing burden
Deep is the wound of my heart

My breast is bursting, my heart is torn
Like the iris you have taken to the graveyard

My yearning for you does not abate
Tell me, why have you deserted me?

You are a fragment of my heart
A lotus withered and decayed

My narcissi are drooping low
Where are you lying asleep?

Your voice still rings in my ears
Tell me, where should I call you?

With musk I will anoint your black curls
And spend hours chatting with you'

Yaqub kept crying for his lost son
His eyes dimmed, he went blind

~

*The merchants take Yusuf to Egypt to sell him in the
market where Zulaykha recognizes him.*

To sell him, they brought Yusuf to Egypt
For three days they hid him from all eyes

But who has hidden the sun or the moon?
They cut through a thousand curtains

Soon Yusuf became the talk of the town
Egypt became like the port of Surat

Bidders thronged to try their luck
The king too sought to make a bid

They took him for a dip in the Nile
Yusuf began to preen and comb

As he loosened his hair to comb
The sight drove the Nile crazy[155]

Seeing his hair scattered on his face
The moon hid itself behind the clouds

With his cupped hands he sprinkled water
It was like a beauty scattering pearls

As he unfurled his long tresses
His owner rejoiced and bragged:

'Who can buy such a priceless thing?
A viper tress has raised its hood

His silvery forearms and bright chest
Are pure and spotless like a lustrous mirror'

As Yusuf added to his adornment
The owner was struck with greater awe

Then he put on a splendid robe
And bloomed like a lovely rose

As Yusuf was raised high on a pavilion
The king lost his heart to him

All lovely people flocked the spot
To get a glimpse of this dashing boy

Though it was a cloudy day in Egypt
His beaming face became a shining sun

His radiance dispelled all darkness
A crowd cried, 'God save us!'

His face outshone the glaring sun
No one had seen a face like that

A great multitude witnessed his splendour
One among the countless was Zulaykha

On her first glance at Yusuf's face
She stood frozen, then gave a cry

'He is the one who has transfixed me!
He is the one whose vision I had!

No words can convey the depth of my sorrow
Will he ever become my glowing candle?

The very face that stole my heart!
Can I have him close to me?

His speech is elixir to me
They bestow immortality

The lives of lovers hinge on their beloveds
His pleasure is my life, his displeasure my death

How many ailing people will be cured
If he just lifts his downcast narcissi!

I have no desire for gold and jewels
A glance from him is enough for me'

She kept rehearsing her tale of longing
'Will he ever know my craving?

He has permeated my whole being
But I dare not betray my secret

If the two of us become mates
I will bare my heart to him

He flashed on me when I was seven
My desire has since sought fulfilment

Great God, grant me one wish!
Make him pine and sigh for me!

Could I buy him on the market?
And never ever be parted from him!

Longing for him my wits have flown
Would that I drive him crazy too!

Does he know how crazed I am?
He is the candle, I the moth

He has filled my bosom with fire
And slain me most ruthlessly

Sharing my woes is no use to me
Only the sufferer knows the pain'

She rent her garment with her hands
And swooned raising a rueful cry

Mahmud, wind up her sorrowful tale
Harping on it will make you sadder

~

*A woman named Bibi Rābia falls in love with Yusuf
who explains to her the true meaning of love.*[156]

O lovers, devotees of form, awaken
Find the essence hidden in appearance

If I divulge to you the meaning of form
Like an infidel you will bow to the idol

The lover has to brace up for the beloved's tyranny
Loving the rose petal, the bulbul attains perfection

Like the moth circling the candle
Aim for nothing but self-immolation

Yusuf's owner brought him out to sell
He put a blazing fire amidst a crowd

His splendour pulled many an anguished soul
All craving for a glimpse of Canaan's moon

One of these was Rabia of Ād tribe
Whose fame as a gnostic had spread far

Crazed and melted by love's raging fire
She had lost all rest and tranquillity

For long, her tearful eyes were fixed on him
'Cruel love, your viper tresses leap upon me

Tell me, who gave you such beauty?
Is this all or does He have more?

Who has embroidered your bone-china face?
Is this a spectacle in China or Badakhshan?

Who gave you these brows and eyelashes?
They shoot a barrage of arrows at my heart

Who poured wine into your narcissus cups?
Yourself drunk, why do you make me tipsy?

Musk from Khutan? Who gifted you that?
An unwary dame is caught in your snare

Who has gifted you with twisted curls
Which drive the young and old crazy?

O adroit charmer with teeth like a string of pearls!
And your lips sweeter and redder than tulips

Who has dug a deep well in your cheek?
Up to my head I am drowned in it

Hasn't the bulbul lacerated his heart
And flaunted his brand to the rose?'

Yusuf grasped the state of her soul
And imparted to her subtle points of love

'Stay a moment and listen to the eternal secrets
In the beginning was peerless, formless Essence

I am a but a drop from His ocean of light
Lesser by a ray than His sun of beauty'[157]

She said:
'Unveil your sunny cheek for me
Put me under your debt forever'

He said:
'The sun is just a speck of His beauty
Forget my appearance, look to my essence'

Though herself the beholder and the beheld
Yet she was far away from knowing herself

She was the lover and the beloved
Herself the *qibla* and *namāz*[158]

He said:
'God created countless spirits in the world
Pure from blemish like spotless mirrors

The "Hidden One" could not brook self-concealment
He took a mirror and got engrossed in Himself[159]

You can see Him in lovely curls and dusky moles
A single beauty manifests in myriad forms

A million mirrors reflect Him alone
Matter and spirit, within and without

When face to face with an appearance
Leave the husk, catch the kernel within

Forms infinite have a single core
In the beginning there was just one

Forms will decay, come what may
Fix your eyes on meaning's core

Choose a love which will ever be yours
Love Him who will live eternally'

As soon as Rabia imbibed this advice
Love's axe fell on her cypress body

She said:
'Now I pass beyond your love
And relinquish all my wealth

Rise and show me your moon-like cheek
I will carry the burden of your debt forever

I know the essence from the appearance now
I have washed off my hands other than Him'[160]

Then she bid farewell to Yusuf
And settled on a spot near the Nile

Having realized her own truth
She gave away all her wealth

Her floor now was covered with ash
Her pillow now was a hard stone

She renounced her desires and put on rags
And daubed her body with the musk of ash

She gave up all earthly attachments
And began to fathom the mystery of union

For some days more she lived on
Absorbed into the Divine Essence

Lovers, learn manliness from her
Sacrifice all for the highest goal

Come and embrace love's sorrow
And taste the ache of separation

Jāmi had told this tale of Zulaykha
Gāmi says the same in Kashmiri

~

Zulaykha buys Yusuf

As Yusuf's beauty stirred up a tumult
Many a buyer thronged to the market

One of the bidders was an old woman
Bent with age like a crooked bow

Carrying a cotton ball, she cried, 'O people
For this cotton ball I will purchase Yusuf!

You own pearls, jewels and rubies
I have nothing but a shard of cotton

You possess glory, power, loads of musk
I own nothing but my restless soul

A lover has no use of worldly things
Gold and silver are of no value to her

Perchance my passion makes my Lord
Grant me a place among immortal lovers'

The old woman's bid stunned Zulaykha
Envying her passion, she began to cry

She bought her love for a kingdom's price
Behold, a love with the partridge gait!

With care and love she brought him home
And began unburdening her heart to him

'I had your vision when I was seven
Living with the nobleman was a mere ploy

You lured me with a false promise
Seeking you out, I reached Egypt

Endless waiting has worn me thin
Frantically I have roamed the streets

Let us be together and exchange love
Let us seize the day and be merry

Love has stabbed every inch of my body
From top to toe I am weltering in wounds

I want to pull you into my embrace
Under the shower of flower petals'

Seeing Zulaykha, Yusuf hides himself
She keeps crying, he turns a deaf ear

'My lord, make yourself at home
Shower love on me from morn to eve'

Yusuf was quick to grasp her trap
Abashed, he turned away from her

She said:
'See, my kohl-rimmed eyes have dimmed
Tell me what makes you so averse to me

I dwell in the hearts of many a prince
At my feet they shed tears of blood

My heart has spurned all except you
You are the one I have always desired

For this alone did I purchase you
I am an eclipsed moon, brighten me!

Swear an oath on your bud-shaped mouth
Utter a word, why this torment?

Sting me with your snake-like tresses
Gaze on me with your drunken eyes

Swear an oath not to avert your gaze
This longing is eroding my woeful soul'

Decked gorgeously, she cornered him
And lured him into her chamber

'Be pleased with me,' she kept pleading
Mahmud, listen to her beseeching now

～

Zulaykha pleads with Yusuf in her chamber

'O moon of Canaan, my soul's comfort!
Cure my vexation, show me kindness

I am heartbroken and much wronged
I, Zulaykha, your frenzied lover

I am a wearied soul, heed my bewailing
You are my anchor, my heart's consoler

My heart is aflame from a baneful parting
Look lovingly straight into my eyes

How much more should I implore you?
Save my honour with a doting gaze

Your pale eyes have made mine sickly
Life without you is a bane to me

I am teetering on the brink of collapse
And have drifted afar from my home

I am on the edge, hear my plea
I put myself at your mercy

Your drunken eyes have made me tipsy
Honour and prestige mean nothing to me

My heart is shackled by your hair strands
A kiss and an embrace are what I desire

The fire of sorrow has burnt me down
A cringing beggar is at your door

O hermit, so calm, don't toy with me
Come, let's get busy in amorous play'

Mahmud, how well have you told this tale!
In Zulaykha's guise you have espied the Beloved[161]

Zulaykha continues her lament

'What twist will love's predicament take?
Why was I, a lovesick woman, ever born?

Ah, why not dead as soon as I was born!
So that I left no tales behind me

Chasing you, I am a waning moon
And a butt of ridicule for my craziness

Shun this obstinacy, my head is on offer
For your sake I have scorned all treasures

On love's shop I paid your price
O my winsome, swinging cypress!

Your shadow is a boon to my eyes
Pray, don't craze me any more!

Shun, for God's sake, your nonchalance
Don't you have a pitying heart?

Chasing you, I have reached here
Now I will have no excuses, dear

These walls are secure, shun all fear
No stranger has an entry here'

Listen to poor Mahmud's wails
His wonderful gift of telling tales

~

'O Turkish archer with arched brows
I am slain by your bows
I will trade Khurasan and India
For a single strand of your hair

If Love unveils itself
as much as a hair's tip
No Zoroastrian or Sheikh
No infidel or Christian will survive!'

~

*Zulaykha begs Yusuf to relent. Failing to seduce him,
she runs after him and tears off a piece from his shirt.
At the door she finds her husband and immediately
puts the blame on Yusuf.*

'Your love, my dear, made me
Abandon my kith and kin

Alas, the writ of destiny has undone
A young and ingenuous girl![162]

Shun your pride and self-conceit
The world has other beauties in plenty

You took my heart, now eye my life
Don't sulk, I will give you my soul

I tied my doleful heart to you
What good was it buying you?

I have reaped only disgrace
I am routed and dispossessed

Command me and I shall obey
Wait expectantly at your door

My heart bears a fiery brand
Like a tulip, in your love

You drive me insane
I am lost to myself

In you I see no grain of pity
Behold my woeful state

O coquettish mischief-maker!
Your brows are spilling blood

You have a graceful delicate body
What grudges do you harbour?

I know you are vain and self-admiring
Proud of your beauty and chasteness

But let us renew our pledge of love
And revel in draining wine cups

Your finger tips are henna-dyed
How many more have you waylaid?

You have cheeks like jasmines
And hands and feet like nosegays

Give me a straight Turk-like look[163]
And I will brag about it ever after

Passion's fire and tears have commingled
Your absence is an unbearable ache

Your ringlets have enmeshed my heart
Come and resolve my predicament

Shamed by your stately stature
The cypress is stuck in mud

How then can I, a poor soul
Flee to a screening shade?

I am wasting away for you
Listen, don't dodge me thus

You have ruined a lovely maid
Writhing in your love's snare

My rooms are decked with jasmine
My cups are brimming with wine

Bathed and preened, I wait here
O tulip, make merry with a jasmine!

My humours are thrown out of balance
By God, my heart is enamoured of you!

Love's flame has engulfed my cotton ball[164]
My patience is all but spent now

No more dallying by you!
No more waiting by me!

Today I must have you
Whether you say "yes" or "no"

I am dry of lip, burnt in soul
My bosom offers you wine cups'

Yusuf gazed above and below
The lovers stood face to face

Desire flared up in his heart too
Her mole and curls had done the trick

Tears streamed from the eyes of both
One hurrying, the other prevaricating

He felt overwhelmed and lost repose
'O poor me, a lowly slave!' he cried

'You have darkened my bright day
And eclipsed my shining morn

What's that you keep in your bosom?'
'My all-knowing God,' he said

With this he took to his heels
Dodging her outstretched hands

'O God, nothing is hidden from you
Your wisdom encompasses everything

You transcend all our description
Honour and might belong to You'

Saying this, he fled from her chamber
Like a graceful swinging cypress

He dashed out as if in a frenzy
Like a fawn sprinting and swerving

She was a snuffed-out candle
Leaping wildly after him

She grabbed his shirt from behind
And tore off a long shred from it

She found her husband at the door
And suddenly started wailing

'Judge between me and Yusuf
Or else I will fret to death

I had retired to my chamber
Where no one has any access

But Yusuf had sneaked in quietly
Drunk, and bent upon some mischief'

An infant, only three months old
Cried out: 'Yusuf is pure, innocent

Check his shirt, it's torn from behind
A proof of his spotless character'

Mahmud, see how she contrived a trick
And fell a victim to her own mischief

She had Yusuf sent to the prison
Thrown at the mercy of the jailers

Away from the garden, the nightingale wails
Away from the beloved, the poor lover wails

~

Another song.

'Why, O reveller, did you flee from me?
Come to me, please do not flee!

Love's chain has impaled me
Come to me, please do not flee!

I am devastated by your love
And ruined by Fate's decree

I am gripped by your thoughts
Come to me, please do not flee!

Blood gushes forth from my eyes
With cups I keep waiting for you

You are my rose, I your iris
Come to me, please do not flee!

You fled and made my heart vagrant
Speak a word and relieve my plight

I, a lovely narcissus, am meant for you
Come to me, please do not flee!

A thief sneaked in and stole my coyness
But you burnt down my desire to ashes

Sharp as flints are your eyelashes
I have offered my heart to them

My heart now is a battered piece
Come to me, please do not flee!

My great craving is yet unfulfilled
If I don't see you, I will surely die

Your arched brows are curved daggers
Come to me, please do not flee!

Where should I wait for you?
You have made me a wanderer

Fate's chain has fettered my neck
Come to me, please do not flee!

I am dishevelled like your hair
Smitten with your gazelle eyes

Even the fawns have hid in the jungle
Come to me, please do not flee!

Come, enjoy my burgeoning youth
My jasmine is turning pale and dull

Why did you turn my gold to brass?
Come to me, please do not flee!

Piqued so much that you hide yourself
O love with tresses like soft hyacinths!

For you I will have a velvet floor
Come to me, please do not flee!

You are my sun, I your moon
Why have you doused my love's flame?

Soon we will vanish under dark clouds
Come to me, please do not flee!'

Thus sang Zulaykha in her chamber
Enticing Yusuf through myriad ways

'My childhood love, don't break your oath
Come to me, please do not flee!'

~

O Love, Mahmud hankers after you!
Unveil yourself to him just once

May the Prophet intercede for me!
Come to me, please do not flee!

~

Zulaykha invites the ladies of Egypt to a feast. Yusuf is sent to the prison.

Soon the story of her desire spread like fire
Yusuf's chastity became the talk of the town

Every lady in the city wagged her tongue
Soon Zulaykha became a laughing stock

'Arrows of illicit love riddle her breast
An anguished soul is her obsession now

Infatuation has torn her modesty's veil
Alas, she has fallen for her Jewish slave!

She spurned her own people for this boy
And squandered all her wealth on him

We hear he's not cast a look on her
Was there no one else except this boy?

If he were to be with us for a while
Like a moth he would circle around us'

When Zulaykha heard the gossip of the town
Her heart was ablaze, she hatched a plot

She dispatched invitations to all rich ladies
And arranged a banquet with music and song

She decked Yusuf with a golden crown
And made him wear the finest silver rings

Jewels of Badakhshan adorned his lovely throat
He gleamed in gold, silver and exquisite pearls

Handed a golden basin and a silvery pitcher
He was asked to enter the ladies' gathering

Each one was given a knife to cut fruit
Yusuf's lustre fell on them like lightning

Their hearts were plunged in pure ecstasy
Utterly perplexed, they sliced through their fingers

Zulaykha won their applause, they all cried:
'Yusuf is indeed the king of all beauties'

When the moon-faced Yusuf threw radiance around
Zulaykha was absolved of all gossip and slander

'A glimpse of his visage has slain her
Love's sword has ripped her moon'[165]

Love, sometimes, is a treacherous game
Many have been trapped by its cunning

Alas, Yusuf too fell a prey to love's treachery!
They schemed to throw him into prison[166]

The world took fright at this treachery
The one professing love had ruined him

In prison Yusuf prayed ardently to God
And gave hope to many prisoners

His kind words, beaming face and manners
Made the warden cherish him like his son

Meanwhile, Zulaykha kept weeping ceaselessly
Her heart was torn between love and prestige

Secretly, she would come to see Yusuf
Wondering how he could gain freedom

'My ill luck, how long will I endure this!
I have lost him, why did I act so foolish?'

Years rolled by till full seven were past
All these years Yusuf was a prisoner

~

*The King of Egypt has a dream and Yusuf is released
from the prison.*

One night the king had a perplexing dream
Of which he could make no head or tail

He inquired its meaning from the scholars
It was a riddle no one could read

Then a servant remembered Yusuf
He told the king of his rare gift

'O king, Yusuf alone can interpret your dream'
The king ordered his release from the prison

A royal horse was sent to bring him
He was freed and others with him

Before the king he stood quite unfazed
'Tell me the dream you have seen'

'I saw seven fully ripened heads of grain
Swallowed by other seven unripe ones

Then I saw seven fat and sleek cows
Devoured by other seven gaunt ones'

Yusuf said, 'For seven consecutive years
Even stones will yield fruit in your land

These will be the years of great abundance
Men will tire piling the heaps of corn

After this, there will be seven years of famine
Rains will stop, drying up rivers and streams

The blazing sun will parch all plants
Intense heat will scorch their fruits

Hunger will drive birds into cages
Hunger will rend father from son'

Yusuf thus interpreted the king's dream
Whose mind was gripped with anxiety

'O my people, we have no succour
Save God, so beseech his clemency'

Terror-stricken, the king died soon after
Leaving Yusuf in charge of his kingdom

The years of plenty banished hunger
Each soul had a basket full of bread

Yusuf's wisdom won him great applause
Announcements were made throughout Egypt

'Those who have the stocks, let them eat
From a variety of vegetables as they please

But keep storing each year for the next
Forget envy, hatred and mutual strife'

Famine struck, wells and springs dried up
The great scarcity killed a father or a son

Gardens and orchards became desolate
Palm trees shed their leaves due to heat

Death was rampant, visiting many households
Only those who had stored enough survived

Yusuf built himself a raised tower
Where he sat on a window everyday

People thronged to catch his glimpse
Even the starving souls felt satiated

His resplendent face emitted godly light
Parched souls got drunk on his sweet juice

A mere glimpse of his inebriated them
He made them forget their thirst and hunger

People came to him from everywhere
And all benefited from his munificence

~

Yusuf's half-brothers reach Egypt in search of food grains. He immediately recognizes them and resorts to a stratagem to bring his brother (Benjamin) from Canaan.[167]

News of a generous king reached Yaqub
Quickly he dispatched his ten sons to Egypt

The king was informed of their arrival
He summoned them for a hearing

'Who are you?' Yusuf asked them
'Sons of Yaqub; we used to be twelve

Now only eleven, one was eaten by a wolf
Which pounced on him and carried him away

Our father has wept ceaselessly for him
His son's sorrow has snatched his sight

We are ten, the youngest is at home
He too set out but father called him back

His she-camel, though, we brought with us
She is lean and cannot bear much load'

Yusuf knew them and conceived a stratagem
Called his manager and gave him instructions

'Give them eleven camel-loads of grain
One sack should be put on every camel

After you have filled their sacks with grain
Hide the measuring cup on the leanest one'

The manager did as he was commanded
Secretly he hid the cup in one of the sacks

Brothers took their measure of grain and rode off
Accused of theft, they were recalled from a distance

Yusuf asked, 'Whose she-camel is this one?'
He is a thief and will be my bondsman

Only he will be detained, others can go
Read the law in the scripture which states so'

The king was stern in his command
'Go and get him whose camel this is'

Taken aback, brothers made a plea
'King, he's far away, give us respite'

They left their grain and travelled home
Wondering how to face their aged father

'Father, send your son, or we lose all
The cup was retrieved from his camel

We begged the king to show us mercy
He was gracious not to detain one of us'

Father said, 'My son is no thief
Why should I send him with you?

I still bear the scars of your old treachery
When I trusted you with my dearest son

Now this one is my only support
A blind man's stick in the dark

I have suffered long and grievously
Don't deprive me of my guiding light'

Finally, seeing no way out, he relented
'Yusuf leaves me again today,' he cried

They brought their brother before Yusuf
A glance on him gladdened his heart

~

Their dinner was placed on five tables
Each for two, it was a sumptuous meal

In a corner the youngest one was sobbing
The king drew him near, 'What's wrong?'

'O noble king, I miss my brother
He's long dead, I am alone

If he were alive, we would sit together
And enjoy your delicious meal'

'You desire a brother; come, let's talk'
He held his hand and took him out

And lo, the king's hand felt like Yusuf's!
He rent his cloak and started wailing

'Yusuf, my brother had hands like yours
And he talked the way you talk

His manners were just like yours
Your speech has a ring of his words

His face sweated in the same way
His eyebrows too looked like yours

He had a mole exactly like you have
His curled locks too were like yours

His brows were bow-like, like yours
His mouth too was bud-like, like yours

His chin had a deep well the way you have
His neck was long and upright like you have

He too had sharp, curious eyes
And a protruding forehead like yours

He had a dagger-like nose like you have
And bow-like eyebrows like yours

His fingers too were dyed with henna
His demeanour too was like yours

He too had a cypress-like swinging gait
He too had a mouth like a rosebud

He too shone with a heavenly lustre
He too had earrings like you have'

Yusuf's veins pulsed fiercely with love
Anguished, he heaved a deep sigh

'Be calm, I am your brother Yusuf
But don't divulge this to your brothers'

All the twelve brothers were together now
But only one knew the truth about Yusuf

Then Yusuf showed them the transaction deal
And told them all they did not know

Stunned first, they then cried aloud
The shrill must have echoed in Canaan

This was the moment of contrition and union
'Tell me how does my poor old father fare?'

'Father is alive but bereft of the gift of sight
For you his loving heart has not ceased to pine'

Yusuf had a shirt once worn by Ibrāhīm
He took it out, 'Take this to my father

Tell him Yusuf pays obeisance to his father
And implores him to travel to this land

Tell him to smell my shirt's fragrance
God willing, his eyes will see again'

They came to Yaqub with Yusuf's shirt
'Father, rub this shirt against your eyes'

In an instant, his gazelle eyes were healed
His anguished soul found a sudden calm

'Cheer up, Father, your Yusuf is alive
He is waiting to receive you in Egypt'

With his family, Yaqub set out for Egypt
Yusuf came to give them a royal welcome

Drenched in tears of joy, they met
'See, Father, this is how God plans

Our parting was a part of His providence
Today the conspirators have been shamed'

Union after a long separation tastes sweet
Father and son got the fill of each other's love

The pain of long separation left Yaqub's heart
Yusuf's winsome face was a feast to his eyes

Morn and eve Yaqub thanked his Lord
'My son is back, what else do I want?'

~

Zulaykha's pining continues. She realizes she has been worshipping a false god, breaks her idol, divorces 'duality' and proclaims Yusuf's creed of 'unity'. Her repentance is accepted as Yusuf requites her love. The two are married.

Not many days had passed after this
That Zulaykha's husband passed away

Her passion for Yusuf did not abate
She became aimless and vagrant

Love's burden had bent her back
Nothing except Yusuf obsessed her

Love's affliction took a toll on her eyes
And cries of lamentation wrecked her body

In love's tight grasp, her heart uttered hot sighs
Though young she looked like an old crone

She shut herself in a little hut of stalks and leaves
Brooding, her neck was bent like a hyacinth stem

Her single devotion was to her love
Its fire had consumed her entirely

'I will lie upon your path here
Or follow you wherever you go'

Slowly her lustrous eyes turned white like flint
Once almond-shaped they now became pebbles

If only they could gaze on her sweetheart!
A bowl and a stick became her companions

One day she placed her idol before her
'Why have I suffered you so far?' she asked[168]

'Why have my prayers not been answered?
Why has Yusuf's heart not thawed for me?

Devotion to you has not brought me a smile
I tried to tie an elephant with a strand of hair[169]

You are a stone and no wonder blind
Fie on me for addressing a stone!'

She smashed the idol crying, 'O my dear God
The king and the slave, all are your servants

I shun duality, my biggest error
And seek your refuge, forgive me!

Listen to my wails, turn Yusuf's heart
I am ruined and helpless without him'

Her sorrowful heart prayed in earnest
God accepted her sincere repentance

That very day Yusuf went out for a stroll
When the unwary Zulaykha was passing by

Many souls assembled to have his glimpse
And Zulaykha recognized him by his fragrance

'Mercy, O king of beauties, mercy!
Mercy, O lord of souls, mercy!'

'Who has wronged you?' asked Yusuf
'Give me your whip,' said the old woman

In her hand, the whip instantly became ash
It was love's fire; a puzzle to the novice

'See me later,' said Yusuf to Zulaykha
'I will listen to your plea in the evening'

The king went around and returned home
Late in the night she called at his door

He ordered his servants to bring her in
She broke down when asked who she was

'The woman who sacrificed all for you
Who sold all she had, to pay your price

I am Zulaykha, the grief-stricken lover
One betrayed by you a long time ago'

Overcome with pity, Yusuf broke down
Her woeful sight made him shudder

He related her full story to his father
'This was a lady of unmatched beauty

She is the one who purchased me with gold
A talk of every town in Rome and Syria

She took a fancy to me when she was seven
And offered her bosom for love's shooting darts

Nothing engrossed her except me
Night and day she wept unceasingly

To lure me, she donned silken and velvet dresses
Then, ached by my absence, tore them to shreds

Though she sported serpentine tresses to sting me
Waiting for me her eyes would become bleary

But for the Prophet's piety that protected me
The wily Satan would have wrecked my chastity

I have always averted my gaze from her face
Hurt by that, she had me thrown into the prison

This crone is the same beauty, known as Zulaykha
Of decrepit frame although younger to me in years'

Love's agony is a burden that lovers bear
Lovers need to learn to die before death

Love is the primeval force behind creation
One drunk on it becomes absorbed in God

'You are my master, I am your maid
You are dearer to me than the entire world

For you my sparkling eyes have turned blind
And your love's flame has burnt my heart'

'Say, Zulaykha, what is that you want?'
'I want you and my lost youth back

To every lover, youth and love are priceless
They care little for the wealth of this world

O my heart-throb, I want you by my side!
Youth without you is of no use to me

I have shunned disbelief and embraced your faith
I have done so much for you, do a little for me'

Yusuf turned to God and prayed ardently
'Lord, have mercy, restore her youth to her!'

Instantly, she became a shining celestial being
Much more elegant than she was ever before

She had her beauty and youth restored
A look at Yusuf also banished her grief

Her almond-shaped eyes shone brightly
A houri like her had never been seen

Just then Jibrīl came with a glad tiding
'Heaven decrees that you two are betrothed'

The lover and the beloved attained their goal
They beheld each other without a veil

'A glance at you has cleansed my rusted heart
I have reached my destination through it

Seeing you is like a shower after a drought
Having you now, my bargain has paid off'

Zulaykha had always loved Yusuf most intensely
Now Yusuf too was caught in love's tangle

The tulip was enamoured of the jasmine
Both sipped cups to their hearts' delight

They spent their days in joy and mirth
The garden of their love was in full bloom

When union's shower fell on her love's garden
She quickly forgot all her pangs of separation

'I have had enough of staying away from you
Wherever you go I will follow you there

I owe you a great debt of gratitude
My worthy love, my handsome Yusuf'

The two were clasped in love's warm embrace
The gardener plucked the rose from the bush

Together they prayed and said thanks to God
'O God, rich or poor, we are your servants!'

She was overwhelmed by God's great mercy
'Great God, you turned a hag into a damsel

I had no hopes of winning back my love
God's mercy is infinite, His signs everywhere'

~

Yusuf's death.

Having had his heart's fill of Yusuf
Yaqub, the old man of Canaan, died

Though Yusuf got busy in his rule
He too inched slowly towards his death

He lived for eight years after Yaqub
Then a desire made way into his heart

Now and then he saw his parents in dream
'O balm of our wounds, we yearn for you'

One day when he was chasing a game
At the head of his imposing cavalcade

Jibrīl appeared to him with a message
'O rose petal of Khalīl's garden

Get ready, your time has come
Today you leave your kin behind'

Yusuf bid farewell to his kith and kin
Though a prophet, he still had to die

As he slid his foot in the stirrup
Death's angel brought him an apple

Yusuf smelled the apple and yielded his soul
The retinue returned, raising mournful cries

God's lovers saw him off with ovation
Bearing witness to his pious devotion

Friends gathered to give him a burial
Invoking blessings on God's messenger

Wealth does not avail against death
How many have left empty-handed!

Man is an air bubble in the world
Yet he is puffed up with pride

He rejoices in his wife and children
Blind to the danger in such devotion

'I am the master of my house,' he brags
This, alas, proves to be his undoing!

Mahmud, be quiet now, speak no more
Die unto love and become immortal

~

Zulyakha laments Yusuf's death.

'Did You bring us to the world in vain?'
A voice answered, 'Every soul shall die'

'O anguished soul, stay here a while
Hear the passionate roar of our souls

They know who lose their first love
Male or female, they turn to ash

Losing a beloved makes you groan
And makes you smear your face with ash

My comely love, come back to me
Bare your face for a fleeting glimpse

My soul burns so much it roars
Bruised, I seek a healing touch

For you my soft body is burnt down
I, O Cupid, am now a laughing stock

O love, heed my piteous entreaties
I am vexed in heart, stay a bit longer

I have been spurned, show your face
My handsome, charming Yusuf

Who will hear if I tell my woes?
Like Layla I am trammelled by love

Come to me again, stop this tyranny
I linger here, what do you have against me?

This helpless woman has none except you
It is a godly act to hold a faltering hand'

~

Love is a trickster, its arrow pierces very deep
And death's arrow impales the rich and the poor

Anguished hearts smoulder quietly to ash
And Mahmud remembers his loss today[170]

Mahmud, this world is loyal to none
It ditches the king and the beggar alike

~

When Zulaykha heard of Yusuf's death
Her world turned upside down

She fell down like a wilted rose
And lay unconscious for three days

When she regained her senses
'Yusuf is dead,' rang in her ears

Then began her lamentations
'Hear my call, my Yusuf, come'

~

*Zulaykha's laments grow more intense. She dies on
Yusuf's grave.*

'Where shall I seek you? O heart-ravisher
My Yusuf, O my Yusuf, my dear Yusuf!

Where are you, my childhood love?
Hear my call, my Yusuf, come!

I ask for nothing, shorn of everything
I will set out. If I have you
I will offer you my life
And don a pretty apparel
For you I will search heights and depths
Hear my call, my Yusuf, come!

In vain have I hoped for his return
He wreaks havoc, shows no pity
He was my comforter at every step
Hear my call, my Yusuf, come!

O peerless lover, my delight and pride!
I was a bulbul, you my rose bower
I desire to be one with my love
Hear my call, my Yusuf, come!

Who will hear me, my soulnourisher?
You bear the burden of my blood
What good is a slavegirl without her master?
Hear my call, my Yusuf, come!

Pity, you have laid me waste
like a withered jasmine or iris!
O stately love, I am wasting away
Chronic sorrow has eaten into me
Hear my call, my Yusuf, come!

Where have you gone leaving this abode?
Why did your affection for me sag?
You have ruined me, no, set me ablaze
Hear my call, my Yusuf, come!

Your death makes the sky bend in shame
And my lustrous eyes have dimmed again
Die not yet, my fingers are yet henna-dyed
Hear my call, my Yusuf, come!

Mourning for you, the sun has hidden away
And the world is shrouded in utter darkness
All the world's beauties are busy self-flagellating
Hear my call, my Yusuf, come!

Tyrannous death, enemy of silver-bodied youths!
You carried them off, wound them in shrouds
Where have you buried my Yusuf?
Hear my call, my Yusuf, come!

O death, does pity never touch your heart?
To fill graveyards, you find a pretext or another
Losing one's love is no less than the doomsday
Hear my call, my Yusuf, come!

Your death has turned my warm days to winter
And my glowing youth is struck with plague
Did I deserve to be forgotten thus?
Hear my call, my Yusuf, come!

O my king with an awe-commanding face!
A shining moon among dim stars
Your death has given me a gnawing pain
Hear my call, my Yusuf, come!

Your death has chopped down stately firs
Death drills your heart like holes in a cage
The grief-stricken groan with death's pain
Hear my call, my Yusuf, come!

Death reduces all the vitals to cinders
It makes the fair ones pine in vain
Garlands remain unused in heaps
Hear my call, my Yusuf, come!

Death splits love pairs apart
Death crushes stony hearts
Death sucks all strength from sinews
Hear my call, my Yusuf, come!

O death, the world has seen many graceful men
Full of cravings, they went into their graves
Bereavement strikes in the midst of joy
Hear my call, my Yusuf, come!

Your death has turned the bulbul dumb
And the rose has torn down its mantle
The hyacinth's neck is drooping down
Hear my call, my Yusuf, come!

O death, I am sapped of all strength
Which graveyard did you send Yusuf to?
Life is treachery, I learnt today
Hear my call, my Yusuf, come!

Rot has eaten into my sweet basil frame
And pain has found a place in my heart
Without you it knows no peace
Hear my call, my Yusuf, come!

I, once a summer jasmine, am withered now
Love's morbid fever has wracked me hard
If you leave, I would rather die
Hear my call, my Yusuf, come!

Roses and jasmines still bloom in my garden
My tresses are hyacinths, my eyes narcissi
How beautiful will I look lying on your grave!
Hear my call, my Yusuf, come!'

Like the raincloud she wept on his grave
For long she raised shrieks of pain
'O pitiless love, my heart's ruin!
Hear my call, my Yusuf, come!'

Stretching herself, she clasped his grave
Whispered God's holy name a few times
The love-mad lady then yielded up her soul
Hear my call, my Yusuf, come!

Though death separates many lovers
They return to their true origin
The two were buried next to each other
Hear my call, my Yusuf, come!

Here Mahmud winds up Zulaykha's tale
To give glad tidings to all woebegone lovers
Of fervent breasts, tearful eyes and burnt-up hearts[171]

Bless him with your ardent prayer
Hear my call, my Yusuf, come!

3. Layla Majnun

Majnun and Layla meet each other in school and instantly fall in love.

Praise to Him who created Muhammad
And filled his breast with His love

The world came to be from his light[172]
In the human form he bears the Essence

Now he becomes Layla, now Majnun
Under such pretexts, he robs lovers' hearts

When Majnun was born
He was named Qais

A nurse suckled the auspicious child
And fed him dates, milk and sweets

Even as an infant he was drawn to beauty
And found himself overwhelmed by love

He feasted his eyes on the spectacle of beauty
And beheld its manifestation in every particle

At four he was sent to school
Escorted by servants and classmates

In school there was a lovely girl
Whose brow lit up the surroundings

Her brow outshone the brightest morn
Her beauty thrilled those around her

Her lovely locks circled around her cheeks
Like the serpents curling around a treasure

Her mole was a grain, her tresses a snare's loop
Trapping in it many a houri and fairy

Her coquettish eyes stirred up a commotion
Provocative, sharp and spilling blood

Her body made fun of the fairest jasmine
The eglantine blushed at the flush of her face

Her safflower-like eyes were brimming wine cups
Casting a gloom on all who stole a wink

A rosy face, hyacinth curls and cypress stature
In short, a hundred doomsdays for the heartsick

The girl was known by the name Layla
Some thought her a fairy, others a houri

Qais's wits went awry at the first sight
Engrossed in her, he forgot his lessons

Her image got etched in him like an inscription
Her presence in school made him ill at ease

A complete hush fell on him as he gazed her face
'What's behind the beauty's form?' he wondered

In her absence he wept grievously
Layla had agitated his young heart

Both began to steal glances at each other
Love's flame had licked their young bodies

When together, they pored over the Quran
And stole a few moments to exchange a word

For him, her face was the scripture's fresh page
Her skewed glances were the strokes of *jeem*[173]

As love suddenly unveiled its visage to them
It made them drunk with the wine of longing

And as it made a place in their hearts
They felt strongly drawn to each other

At the end of the school everyday
They exchanged their writing tablets

Layla would say, 'Do see me later
On that pretext show me your face'

Panting, the lovesick boy would run to her
And sate his passion while returning her tablet

Vexations gripped the frenzied lover
He missed no chance of meeting her

But the simpleton shared this with his mates
And soon the secret became the talk of the town

The classmates reported all to their parents
'Layla and Qais secretly love each other'

People flocked to her mother with advice:
'Call your daughter back from the school

We have news; a youth has fallen for her
Beautiful, graceful, with a face like the moon

From dawn to dusk they rivet each other
Both have lain off their lessons in the school

The whole of Arabia talks about them
"Layla," they say, "is lost to Majnun"'

Her mother rent her garment in frustration
And shot a missive to Layla at school

'Why have you put us to shame in school?
Why do you make our kinsmen sling mud at us?'

Layla came to see her anguished mother
Tore her garment and started grieving

'Preserve your honour to be sought after
Fairy-faced girl, you do not lack suitors

Let your father not get a whiff of it
Or he will chop you into pieces

Woe to the couple who bear a girl child!
She only brings trouble to her parents'

Layla spoke a few soft words to her mother:
'Patience mother, please don't lose your cool!

Tell me, who have I fallen in love with?
Love and hate are both foreign to me

What's this talk about? Tell me again
I beg your pardon, talk straight to me!

A mere look makes me break into sweat
Give me a test in my lessons if you wish

Mother, tell me what is it they call love
How does it feel, what's its truth?

Our enemies have concocted a story
They want a split between you and me

I am an innocent little girl
Oblivious to love's passion'

Layla spoke in earnest, asserting her innocence
Her wit and eloquence had the desired effect

Her mother was now satisfied
She thought her daughter innocent

Still Layla was to remain captive
Within the walls of her house

She cried, 'I staked everything for a single desire
My Majnun, how can I send you a word?'

And wept, 'My frenzied lover, my friend
Where are you? I will die crying for you!'

Mahmud's heart too inclines to love
Like the two lovers in thrall of each other

~

Layla sings a song.

'My Majnun, my frenzied lover
Say, where shall Layla wait for you?

O my love, busy in reading from the tablets
How elegant you look in the midst of pupils!
Like the moon sitting among stars
Say, where shall Layla wait for you?

I am shackled, my youth is wasting away
Fearing disgrace, parents have shut me in
I will deck my curls and ears for you
Say, where shall Layla wait for you?

O merchant at the port of Surat[174]
Give them a slip and come to me
I will lay down my life for you
Your lips are rosy, your teeth pearls
Say, where shall Layla wait for you?

The blaze of separation has reduced me to ashes
Give me a glimpse of your face in secret
Alas my childhood, my innocent youth!
Say, where shall Layla wait for you?

Now smouldering quietly, now burning fiercely
You have wrought havoc on me
O my lover of fame, I endure infamy
Say, where shall Layla wait for you?

Love's malady, friend, has no cure
Where can I flee from its clutches?
I am your sacrifice, hear my plaint
Say, where shall Layla wait for you?

Without me you are an aimless wanderer
I too am distraught without you
I long to see you once more
Say, where shall Layla wait for you?

If I knew the way, I would run after you
Now you find a way to see my misery
O moon-faced love, forget me not!
Say, where shall Layla wait for you?

O Sayyid Amīr's pearl necklace[175]
Let's enter the garden together
And learn the lessons of the Quran again
Say, where shall Layla wait for you?

My robust frame is crumbling down fast
My snake-like tresses are shrivelling up
We won't come to this world again
Say, where shall Layla wait for you?

My nights are spent numbering the stars
You leave my heart and soul numb with cold
Pining for you, I don't sleep a wink
Say, where shall Layla wait for you?

Your sweat-soaked eyebrows are crescents
arching gracefully the stars below
Mahmud harbours a strong desire of you
Snatch a moment to show up once
Say, where shall Layla wait for you?'

~

Majnun becomes distraught, pining for Layla.

When Qais found himself parted from Layla
He turned ashen with love's soreness

In frenzy he would run to school
The lovesick boy would call out her name

'Where is my love gone?' he would cry
'Her crazy lover is undone without her'

He resolved upon feigning blindness
To steal her glimpse in a beggar's guise

He took off his robe and put on rags
And smeared his body with dust and ash

For love's sake he faked blindness
Took a cup and set out for Layla

He entered her courtyard raising a cry
Perchance they take him to his love!

Love's vexation had overwhelmed him
He stumbled, the cup broke into pieces

He started crying even louder
Lamenting over the broken cup

Majnun sings a song at Layla's door

'A lion then, a jackal now[176]
Woe to my half-baked cup!

I have lost all in this bargain
Love's thief has ruined me
How can I bear love's pain?
Woe to my half-baked cup!

I offer you my head, come as a guest
Look for yourself, what I have gone through
A falcon is caught in a snare
Woe to my half-baked cup!

For you I will efface myself
I lost my way in the middle
I would have made you nosegays
Woe to my half-baked cup!

Look for an augury in the book of love
Banish my darkness with your moon
Where, O love, should I look for you?
Woe to my half-baked cup!'

~

Majnun's craziness becomes more intense. His parents plead with him to return home. The two lovers continue to pine for each other.

Layla saw the cup was a subterfuge
She knew he had no need for alms

'O mother, don't you know this
Giving alms with your hands is best'

On this pretext, she met the crazed lover
With a cup full of jewels and coins

She took him by hand and helped him stand
Pleading with him, expressing her love

'O madman, why do you stay away?
What alms do you want, ask me?'

'I want my cup back,' said he
And started relating his woeful tale

She said, 'My each fibre is infused with your love
Visit my house in this guise again and again'

This way Majnun met his sweetheart
But the meeting left him more uneasy

For long they were lost in each other
There was an outcry as the news spread

Layla's tribe rose up against him
He was beaten black and blue

Now he was lost to himself and the world
That fairy's love had deranged his mind

The news was carried to Sayyid Amīr
Whose eyes shed blood for his son

'He has retired to desolate places, bareheaded
Shedding tears all the time for Layla's sake'

Sayyid Amīr rushed to see his frenzied son
He found him asleep, torn with anguish

He saw his cloak torn to shreds
His breast ablaze with love's flame

His dear son was reduced to ashes
Crying ceaselessly day and night

His shoulders bore the marks of lashes[177]
The sight broke the father's heart

'O vision of my eyes, my son
Who ensnared you in school?

Which black snake has coiled around you?
Who smeared your jasmine body with dust?

Whose black snaky curls caught your fancy?
Like a black viper you stung me and left[178]

Drunk on love's wine you lost all sense
Come back home, don't be sullen'

'What's your name?' Majnun queried
'Where are you from, why do you raise such cry?'

'Am I not your father?' asked his father
'Majnun, come back home to live with us'

'I have no concern with father or mother
Layla, my love, is the only thing I desire

If you're my father, show me Layla
If you cannot, stop bothering me'

Father said, 'Listen, O apple of my eyes
If you want Layla, be calm and listen

If you want to have her glimpse
Come home without any delay'

Majnun agreed and returned home
His mother held him in embrace

Be all ears, my beautiful earring
I will rock you in the cradle again

My bosom is riddled with a hundred holes
Loveless son, you didn't look back once!

Pangs of a mother's love are still fresh with me
Whose collyrium eyes have cast a spell over you?

Do not abandon your helpless parents
Tell your secret, what's our fault?

Are you not the vision of my eyes?
Are you not my only hope in old age?

Give up craziness and stay with us
I will fetch you a fitting match

The world perishes fast, nothing remains
Why, my son, are you so adamant?

To pursue women is no sign of manliness
They turn your tulip cheeks sick and sallow'

'Marriage means nothing to me
I only want my beloved, Layla'

Majnun, a Cupid, was forced to wear fine clothes
And admonished sternly for his misdemeanour

'Why do you bring us such disgrace?
Let alone serve, you have betrayed us

In old age we had great expectations of you
Thought you would support our crumbling frames

You would take our place when we are gone
Someone lured you and you deserted us

If you abandon us, we will follow you
Offer you our lives, sacrifice our souls

A childless man faces neglect while alive
Despite riches he is counted worthless

A childless man gropes blindly in the dark
Despite all, he remains uncared for

A childless man finds no helping hand
As he grows old, he meets with abuse

He is like a leftover fruit on the tree
Blown away when the wind turns fierce

No one lends him a sympathetic ear
Vainly he wishes for a helping hand

No one awakes him from his sleep
And no one lulls him to pleasant dreams

Eid and *Herath* bring no joy to him[179]
Like a tramp he seeks shelter in mosques

No one attends to him in distress
Vainly he waits for someone to come

No one overlooks his shortcomings
Vainly he looks for someone to talk to

He looks wistfully towards all
Vainly he waits for some help

This is the plight of a childless man
Save God he has no true friend'

Majnun said, 'Father, this dilemma is insoluble
Parents cannot substitute one's beloved

Remember, you had promised me Layla
Pining for her my moon is eclipsed

If I don't have her, I will flee from you
My heart is stolen; I will give up the world

Shedding blood, my eyes have frozen
My limbs are sagging, I can't stand

My back is crooked due to love's burden
Shedding tears, my eyes have lost vision'

A doctor was called, he wrote a prescription
'Dispatch somebody to Layla's court

Let him go and gather some dust carefully
From nowhere but Layla's own windowsill

Tell him Layla has heard his lamentation
And sent him the collyrium of her eyes

Applying it will cure his ailing eyes
Tell him she wants to see how he fares'

Fine dust was brought to Majnun
And given to him as Layla's gift

He put it in his eyes at once
News from Layla lit him up

Thinking that Layla would arrive soon
His tearful eyes looked around expectantly

'Will she be struck by my kohl-rimmed eyes?
How can I retain it, tears wash away the kohl?'

When tears welled up into his eyes
He held them back with great effort

To stem their flow, he shut his eyes forcefully
But heart's blood burst through his bosom

Bleeding, he fainted on the ground
What men had heard, they saw it now

Everyone was convinced beyond doubt
Indeed, it is Layla he is enamoured of

Meanwhile, Layla's friends found a way to her
And maidens gathered to share her grief

Somebody related to her Majnun's state
And Layla was struck with melancholy

A doctor was called to examine her
'Layla is torched by the fire of love'

They pricked her vein, blood oozed out
It fell on the ground, writing 'Majnun'

'If you wish Layla alive and healthy
Bring her the real medicine, love's union'

The same day Majnun took to wilderness
Shedding tears from his lustrous eyes

Suddenly, his elbows started bleeding
Striking the onlookers dumb with wonder

What they witnessed was truly amazing
The spilt blood turning into Layla's name

'O mad lover, how come this blood flows?'
'Majnun and Layla are not separate,' he replied

There they punctured her vein, here he bled
Listen, fakirs, this is what you call love

The two bodies had but one soul
The men of devotion call this 'oneness'

~

Song

Deem not love a trivial matter
Love holds the highest station

Love makes the lovers forget food and drink
Love drives them to the forests and caves

What befell Farhād because of love!
It made him cut through the mountain

Sheikh San'ān was smitten with a Hindu girl
Passion for her made him keep her piglets

Love devastated poor Zulaykha
Love caused her abject misery

Love did not spare Sultan Mahmud[180]
His beloved was Ayāz, his slave

Love drove Majnun to Najd's mountains
And made him wail day and night

Love surges inside Mahmud's breast too
Like it surged within both Qais and Layla

~

Majnun visits Layla in the disguise of a ram in a flock of sheep driven by a shepherd.

Majnun stopped to eat, drink and sleep
Wandering in jungles, bemoaning his pain

The crazed lover was plunged in love's sea
Just then he spotted a shepherd with a flock

The flock was grazing in Layla's meadow
Majnun went running to the shepherd

'O Shepherd, whose flock is this?'
'It belongs to Layla,' he replied

'Shepherd, grant me a request
Let me attend to it for a while

Or drive me along to Layla's place
Let me mix up with the mute sheep'

The shepherd saw his swarthy parched lips
And offered him a cup of milk

'Shepherd, my bosom is ablaze with love
I am consumed by the desire to see her

Let me put on a ram's skin
And mix with these animals

Shepherd, will you lend me one
And take me to her in disguise?'

The shepherd said, 'I will stand by you
Will you put a ram's skin on your soft body?

Will your wrecked body make it to her?'
'Union will cure me,' said Majnun

'I have a fresh sheep skin
Which I am loaning to you

Go and put it on your body
Get well soon, O lovesick man!'

Majnun took off his robe
And put on the ram's skin

The shepherd pulled the skin down his neck
Majnun's skin was bruised by stones

He started crawling on all the four
Love's passion spurred him on

By evening he reached Layla's courtyard
And with the flock he entered fearlessly

As Layla heard the bleating of the sheep
She came out running from inside

Soon she began to observe the animals
Looking closely for a human face

She went in front of each animal
Till she spotted a human in a ram's guise

Layla touched his shoulder with a supple stick
He trembled to the core and gave out a shriek

A ram from the flock was kept aside
She had recognized him in his guise

'My love, put aside the ram's guise
Let me caress your aching body

Your disguise adds salt to my wounds
Cast it away or I will tear it down'

Majnun laid aside the skin and gazed at her
His dagger-shaped nose stabbed her heart

Love's axe had fallen on Majnun's heart
And a sane mind had become insane

As Majnun sat near Layla
Love's fire was rekindled

As Layla raised Majnun's drooping head
It was dawnbreak on the eastern horizon

The afflicted lover left with the flock
Mahmud relates love's myriad tales

~

Again, Majnun put on the sheep skin
He never had his heart's fill of Layla

Again, he came in a ram's disguise
And entered Layla's courtyard

Again, the pretty Layla came out
Groping her way with her hands

Searching for him, she was emasculated
Worn out, she finally reached Majnun

'Oh, what am I looking for?
A ram, gazelle or a man?

Someone's gazelle eyes are peering at me
Lost to myself, I am waiting endlessly

Wherefrom has this stranger come?
A man has appeared from nowhere'

She recognized him through his disguise
'Lift this mask, my frenzied lover

Lay bare your face, I want to see you
You make me feel so helpless

In my lap I will caress your head
Make you drink from the union's cup'

She caressed his chest and shoulders
'I will heal your love's wounds with balm

Who has lashed your body with sticks?
My heart breaks to see you suffer

I too am smitten with your desire
I can neither flee nor have rest

My lovesickness surely exceeds yours
Your eyes have indeed bewitched me

May I be your sacrifice!
Why has love slain us both?'

Majnun laid the mask aside
Union led to oneness[181]

They shared the secrets of love together
No one is privy to them save a fakir

Who can spell out what oneness means?
It revealed itself in the guise of Muhammad[182]

Know the Friend through all masks
Behind myriad veils He is one[183]

A shell covers the kernel, the lid hides the secret
Mahmud, know that the Beloved is very near[184]

~

After this union there again was separation
Shedding tears and blood again fell to his lot

Lovelorn, he raised cries of lamentation
Crying copiously like the spring cloud

'Alas, my life has gone utterly waste!
Love, you are to blame if I die

My heart is aflame, my body become ash
Day and night I am weeping ceaselessly

A glimpse of you and this darkness will vanish
My sightless eyes will regain their vision'

He cried and bemoaned his woeful state
'Layla, my love, I didn't value you enough!

My jasmine sheen has turned sallow now
And the glory of my youth is blown away'

~

Song

'O girl, I will follow you everywhere
My dear love, don't treat me with such disregard!

Your hyacinth tresses are exquisitely done
Beautiful curls are coiling around my neck
Who has done your ringlets in this way?
My dear love, don't treat me with such disregard!

Don't hide your spotless radiating moon
How elegant these earrings look on your girlish ears!
Lovers could make their nests in their middle
My dear love, don't treat me with such disregard!

Two brows etched on your moon-like face
Which perfect artist has carved them?
How many lovers have shrivelled up
by your crescent of twenty-ninth night?
My dear love, don't treat me with such disregard!

Like the summer jasmine your youth is in full bloom
I will reveal my secret to you, girl!
Life slips away and death confounds senses
My dear love, don't treat me with such disregard!

Don't be so proud of your moon-like face
Don't flaunt your hair on the crown, O Nāgrāy's Hīmāl![185]
Where will I seek you out, O Gopal, retiring into the
forest![186]
My dear love, don't treat me with such disregard!

Cupid, the god of love, has clothed you in red robes
But these red robes will turn black one day
How many beauties have ended in perdition!
My dear love, don't treat me with such disregard!

Why do you wail? Your resources are plentiful
Your immaculate body deserves a dress from Bengal
Look around, how many has time ruined?
My dear love, don't treat me with such disregard!

Don't leave me to the vagaries of fortune
Or to the mockery of the multitudes
Don't strut hastily bruising my heart
You have cleft me into two
We are all bound to die
My dear love, don't treat me with such disregard!

Majnun is at your door with a plea
My lady, for God's sake show up once
Crimson lotuses adorn your girlish ears
My dear love, don't treat me with such disregard!

My Layla, Majnun entreats you
Your mole has titillated many a lover
Don't toss your viper tresses with such conceit
Let me have a fleeting glimpse of you
My eyes caught you, O black beauty, in pitch dark
My dear love, don't treat me with such disregard!'

Mahmud Gāmi is a supplicant at your door
O moon at its full, hear me for God's sake!
Seize the hour before sorrow finds its way to us
My dear love, don't treat me with such disregard!

~

Majnun's father visits Layla's place and pleads with her father for their marriage. He agrees. The wedding is arranged. Majnun, however, acts outrageously in the assembly and the marriage is cancelled.

As Sayyid Amīr gauged their love's intensity
He called his kinsmen for consultation

They thought over the matter for long
And decided to plead with Layla's father

Together they went to him with this plea
Sayyid Amīr begged him with folded hands

He retorted, 'Your crazy boy is no match for Layla
Fitting that he be held in chains and fetters'

For long Layla's father stood his ground
And declined the pleas of Sayyid Amīr

At last, he relented when the nobles intervened
Both factions cleansed their hearts of misgivings

It was decided that the two will be betrothed
And the two will not be rent apart

Friends and well-wishers geared up
Both tribes agreed on the wedding

Sayyid Amīr said, 'Son, listen to me
Discipline yourself if you want Layla

Give up this frenzy and you will have her
Cups of love's wine will come your way

A well-decked horse is kept ready for you
Cheer up, we are going to bring Layla

Handsome bridegroom, my dear Majnun
Sip a draught and set off with a graceful gait'

Hearing this, Majnun was overjoyed
The name 'Layla' gave him a new life

They tied a golden belt around his waist
Bought with the wealth of India and Samarqand

A multitude lined up row after row
Princes and nobles of different ranks

Men in large numbers were invited
Felicitations poured in from all sides

Trumpets were blown as the assembly grew
Carpets of brocade were spread for them

Prince Majnun stood out among all
Like a star shining on a dark night

Adorned gorgeously, he was escorted
By no less than seventy thousand men

It was like an estate on the move
Joy and merry filled the air

Wet nurses showered blessings on their beloved
Maidens and attendants followed the retinue

Maidens sang joyful nuptial songs
Servants stood with cups in their hands

The hour of the wedding was come
Song and music resonated in the air

Wise men and scholars assembled together
While Majnun's presence delighted Layla

Waiting for the pact to be signed
Anxiety loomed large on her face

The two tribes were at the pinnacle of joy
But God's scheme overrode their plans

Layla's puppy crawled into the gathering
Majnun stood up and lapped it in his arms

Cuddling it, he showered kisses on it
Placed it on his knees and wept

Used its paws to scratch his love's wounds
He felt a balm on his aching wounds

'You are blessed with the sight of Layla's face
Tell her my soul hankers after her

She has filled my heart with love's flame
This separation I can endure no more'

Ashamed at this, Layla's father rose
Wailing and raising a hue and cry

Swords were drawn, the two clans clashed
Plenty of blood was spilt that night

Scholars and clerics fled from the place
Seeing this, Layla was stricken with grief

Her heart was torched, she started wailing
Their ill-starred love was indeed jinxed

Crying profusely, she fainted on the ground
Her jasmine body turned saffron purple

Majnun then took to the Najd mountains
And escaped from the eyes of his kinsmen

Gazelles and stags became his friends
Lions of the jungle became his servants

Layla's remembrance haunted him again
His wails echoed through the rugged mountains

~

Song

No wonder he runs to Najd's forests
Whose heart is stolen by the thief of love

Every moment a storm rages in his breast
Whose heart is stolen by the thief of love

Roses of all types will deck his head
And earlobes bear love's earrings
They will make him drink from longing's tavern
Whose heart is stolen by the thief of love

Seek the essence, cleanse your mirror of rust
The dot of your *ghain* will be erased[187]
He will become privy to the innermost secret
Whose heart is stolen by the thief of love

He will be seated in the midst of the garden
All his grief and worry will disappear
They will call out to him like a bulbul
Whose heart is stolen by the thief of love

Though grief meet him at every step
Like Mansur sitting in the midst of fire

Polished with ash, his mirror will shine
Whose heart is stolen by the thief of love

Gold, not brass, fetches high price
Like a decrepit beggar, sit at His door[188]
Plunge love's dagger into your heart
Whose heart is stolen by the thief of love

Mahmud, hearken to this counsel
Perhaps conceit still holds you in grip
Become a bulbul and fly in the garden
Whose heart is stolen by the thief of love

~

Majnun meets Layla and explains his conduct.

Hearing his wails, Layla unbarred her window
Her eyes were fixated on her lover's path

Majnun reached there with stealthy steps
'Give me your hand, I will come inside'

She dropped a lasso, he jumped in
Both sat together to recite the Quran[189]

'O crazy lover, see what you have done?
Why grumble now, you threw away your chance?

Had you shown a little more caution
Our love would have attained fruition

Why did you lose your mind there?
And leave the assembly in frenzy?'

'Listen, O beauty, to what I say
Love's fire had burnt down my soul

Love's call first rose from the nook of Oneness
The Word was born without mouth or tongue[190]

Love is a treasure hidden in the Word
The Word leads you to the meaning's core

The Word is adornment to the king's throne[191]
Reason is astonished at Love's station

Reason is Love's handmaiden
Love leads to the secrets hidden

Reason is sluggish, Love swift of action
Love is like the king, Reason his vizier

Jibrīl is wonderstruck and knows little
Of how it found a way to God's presence!

Ask God for wholesome Reason
Love annihilates the living hearts

Reason commands "right" to the will
Fakirs call it a slave, no more

Your love has made me quit reason and sense
This is why I am slighted by the men of Reason

If I possessed reason and smartness
I would know the cure for my suffering

The frenzied ones dispense with discernment
They cherish vision more than union'

Suddenly, a rival appeared from nowhere
Drawing a sword to smite Majnun

The lovers' prayer moved the Heaven
His dagger-wielding hand was petrified

Befuddled, he cried in distress
'Your love is pure, forgive me'

Majnun prayed to God on his behalf
His hand was freed from the charm

~

Majnun goes away and enters a beautiful garden
where he stops a woodcutter from cutting a fir tree.

The love-stricken Majnun entered a garden
The brand of separation made his breast roar

The garden was a paradise of wonder
Much like the Garden of Eden

It was full of beautiful houris
Who were quietly making nosegays

Nightingales trod softly on flower petals
Stealing silently the human hearts

In the midst, houris were bathing
Like stars shining in darkness

Streams were filled with flowing water
And flowers had bloomed in plenty

Roses, henna flowers, moss roses and
Morning glories climbed up everywhere

Hyacinths, narcissi and other flowers
Cockscombs and iris too had bloomed

Sweetbrier gave a fiery look
As if burning from love's ache

Cockscombs had grown in abundance
Jasmines, marigolds and red roses too

Tartary flowers, red salvias and sunflowers
All lined up in rows on the stream banks

The garden, in brief, was in full bloom
Flowers of all types had decked its floor

Green grass looked like a velvet carpet
Spread in the midst of the wondrous garden

Wild mynahs warbled on rose boughs
Piercing the hearts of the keen listeners

Bulbuls of many hues sang to the roses
Banishing sorrow from the afflicted hearts

Chinars, it seemed, had come from Paradise
Fresh breeze made them even lusher

Among these, a fresh fir tree also stood
Full of blossoms like a decked bridegroom

Bulbuls chirped on its branches
Flitting from one flower to another

The oriole and the magpie too sang
Cheering up the lovers' hearts

The ringdove trilled the whole night
All sang the glory of the Bountiful God

O Zephyr, watch the crazed lover enter
Into this paradisiacal garden today

The garden's beauty freshened up Majnun's soul
The spectacle of coloured flowers enlivened him

He was overcome by a refreshing sleep
He woke up and set out to saunter

His eye caught a man axing a cypress tree
Chopping its branches from top to bottom

The sight of the cypress touched him to the core
Its lofty stature stirred love's remembrance

'Don't axe my cypress, O woodcutter
Don't wreck my love's stately figure[192]

Hold back your axe, the cypress is innocent
If you want wealth, take it from me'

Majnun got absorbed in the cypress
His delicate body felt bruised and torn

'You are chopping me with your axe
And wracking my youthful body'

Majnun gladly gave him all he had
And saved the cypress from his axe

Alert again, his eyes became bleary once more
He left the garden and took to the Najd jungle

Again, he started crying out to Layla
And endured great agony like Farhād

Truly, love's conflagration had torched him
Listen, Mahmud, how a lover pleads!

~

Majnun sings a song.

'What has piqued you that you hide your face?
Say, O lady, why do you drive us mad?

When you take a dip in the Indus waters
Many hearts go crazy
See, how you tantalize our lovesick hearts!
Say, O lady, why do you drive us mad?

Your jasmine-like hands scatter jasmine petals
And you toss your pretty tresses around
You throw your viper curls to sting us
Say, O lady, why do you drive us mad?

When you open your almond-shaped eyes
No wonder you drive gazelles to the jungle
And your sword-like brows slaughter the lions
Say, O lady, why do you drive us mad?

Sitting in the garden you make nosegays
And make us go around the springs
For whom do you freshen up?
Say, O lady, why do you drive us mad?

Quietly, you string the safflowers
And make bouquets of jasmines
You deck your delicate body with those flowers
Say, O lady, why do you drive us mad?

O houri, swinging your eardrops
You show up like a flash to your lovers
You keep them smouldering, they dread to say!
Say, O lady, why do you drive us mad?'

What are you telling Mahmud Gāmi
Putting such a high price on your youth?
Is there a youth which won't be blighted?
Say, O lady, why do you drive us mad?

~

Layla sings a song.

'How shall I find you?
O cave dweller!
My frenzied Majnun
I will follow you there

I, Layla, decked to perfection
Am waiting for you, my bridegroom!

Roam the jungles or take flight
My pure-hearted frenzied lover
You lured me when I was seven
Now stay a moment, my frenzied lover!

How sore is the sting of misfortune!
Who wrote for me such a grim fate!
I bore with my family's rejection
Stay with me, my frenzied lover!

Come to me, my alluring love
I am wandering in your pursuit
Youth will soon turn into old age
Stay with me, my frenzied lover!

I am a newly arisen moon
Come to me, I feel helpless
Layla is worn out pining for you
O serpent-like frenzied lover
Come to me quietly
Why hide in caves and forests?

My entire youth is wasted after you
My childhood friend, my frenzied lover
Love's sickness is hard to heal
There is no escape from this affliction

You have broken my heart into pieces
O frenzied love of languid eyes
My body aches with a searing pain
You gave me a slip and showed no mercy

Show up, O my blooming rose garden
I stray aimlessly, keep your promise'

Mahmud utters his woeful tale
O frenzied love of worthy name!

~

Layla sets out to look for Majnun in the mountains of Najd.

Layla crossed the mountain to meet her love
And found him prostrate on the ground

She cried out to him, 'What are you up to?'
He heard the shout and began to weep

He recognized her call instantly
'Don't be cross, I offer you my head'

'Layla, I am Majnun, your ill-fated lover'
Like a flame these words scorched her heart

'I have searched these mountains day and night
And covered myself with the garment of taunts

Abashed by my kinsmen and jeered by enemies
Love, I had you once, but now you evade me

Should I say you don't love me enough?
I loved you much; thought you did the same

Enticing love, you have wounded my heart
My love-besotted Majnun, my dearest one!'

She rushed to examine him closely
His breast was blasted with love's ache

For long they cried and bemoaned their lot
Till animals gathered around to console them

Then Layla took his head in her lap
Wailing for her love overcome with sleep

'I deserted my family for your sake
And lost my senses in your pursuit

My state is woeful, no, unspeakable
The web of coyness had strangled me

All my vitals have burnt with love
Away from you, I could only cry

I never dangled my love's eardrops
Consumed as I was by your thoughts

I never did my curly locks
And never wore a fine dress

This body of mine is riddled by you
My back is bent, my weeping ceaseless

My jasmine body looks pale and sick
My burgeoning youth is thunderstruck'

Majnun wept too, 'O my fairy
Your memories have never left me

My body is lacerated by your separation
Let's die together, we will die only once

My nights were spent lamenting your loss
Was there a moment when you missed me?

Here is my heart torn to pieces
If you don't answer, I will die

God knows how you have remembered me
I offer you my head, the only thing I own'

'Without you I have been miserable
A single glimpse was all I sought'

~

Layla has a frightful dream. She thinks Majnun is dead.

As the dawn broke and bulbuls chirped
He said, 'Layla, let's make a move'

He escorted her and brought her home
They then parted till the Judgement Day

They bid farewell to each other
Never to meet again in this world

Thereafter Layla wept for long
Until one night she had a dream

Majnun was dead on a mountainside
Either frozen stiff or in deep sleep

Stags and gazelles gathered around him
Lions of the wild were paying him homage

She woke up, terribly frightened
And couldn't wait more to see him

The dream caused her great dejection
Sorrow turned her tulip face pallid

His thoughts made her weep bitterly
And smear her young body with dust

'We were mates in the school
You left your parents for me

You lost all ease and peace after me
Your bright days turned pitch dark

My eternal love, crushed by sorrow
Where are you? I will cry beside you

I am much taken by you, O fair youth!
I could spend my life gazing your face

Can I comb your tresses with my own hands?
Deprived of your visage, I will surely die insane

O adept lover, you have singed my heart[193]
Given me pain and vanished like a wizard

A rose I was, or an iris, exulting in you
Am now a narcissus despoiled by the bee

A summer jasmine I was, taking pride in you
Am now wilted, withered, fallen dead

Who must have washed and laid you in the grave?
Your parting is worse than burning in fire'

Distraught with melancholy, Layla fell sick
Singing for Majnun dirges of varied kinds

~

'Don't leave me halfway, my frenzied lover
Living away from you is an agony

Ecstasy drove you out of the gathering
You retired to a cave in Najd heroically

Come to me, I beg you, as an honoured guest
Stay for some time, I will give up my kin for you

I feel worthless, uprooted and reduced to naught
Not worth a farthing now, my burden is unbearable

Drain the cups of love's musky wine
Lap me in your arms and take me along

You beguiled me, my heart is your captive now
I am like a fish caught in your locks and mole

Your eyelashes are the spears and darts of love
Like my love's cup, my lovelorn heart is splintered

Where have you lain, how do you fare?
Parted from you, I will wear out crying

Which wine server gave you sip after sip?
Who took off your robes and shrouded you?

O Majnun, where have you gone giving me a slip?
My gazelle, your death will wear me away!

I wish you had frolicked like a fawn
and not walked into the mouth of death!'
Mahmud's passion is ever on a high

~

*Layla dies, followed by Majnun. The romance
concludes on a mystical note.*

She sobbed like this for a long time
Calling Majnun to come to her

She complained to God of her misery
'The sword of grief has ripped my heart

I wish I had Majnun with me
To unburden my heart to him

I wish I could clasp and rock him
Address him by affectionate names'

She kept crying, 'O Majnun, O Majnun!'
She uttered 'Allah' and yielded up her soul

When the news reached Majnun
He came running to clasp her grave

He wept bitterly grovelling in dust
'Dear Layla, what has become of you?

You set yourself early on love's path
Like a moth I will flutter around you

Did you remember me at the time of death?
Alas, how great is my suffering!'

He kept wailing and calling her name
His dirges resonated in the graveyard

Majnun's bereavement was profuse
His love for Layla was pure of lust

He clung to her grave in deep agony
Layla's father too rent his robes

Finally, a call from Layla came to him
God united him with his beloved

The grave split open, he went in
Her beauteous form lay supine

She lay there before his eyes
As if in a deep peaceful sleep

He took her in his arms
And showered kisses on her

Both found a place in the Abode of Heaven
Nothing of this world escapes perdition

The two families mourned their loss
And testified to their chaste love

They recited the *fātiha* and praised God[194]
Everyone was convinced of his purity

Death dulls the lustre of gazelle eyes
It snatches the hopes of kith and kin

Death lays waste many a household
It pushes people into oblivion's abyss

Death snatches one's dear ones
It rends apart the loving pairs

Listen Mahmud to the truth about love
The Real shows through the Apparent's veil[195]

How well have you told love's grievous tale!
How well have you stirred the lovers' hearts!

Know the Essence from the Appearance
Appearance is a veil to be seen through

Make best of the moments of your youth
Everything perishes; we end up in our graves!

4. Sheikh San'ān

Praise be to the Almighty Lord who
Bestowed intelligence on the dust

Praise rendered, the next best thing
Is to send blessings on the Prophet

Now, if you lend me your ears
Love's subtle point I will reveal

Sheikh San'ān attained great fame
But love left him deeply perplexed

A perfect guide for the seekers
Was beset with love's ordeal

A terrible dream shook him
He was kneeling before idols

Waking in utter fright
He called all his pupils

'Friends, I seek God's refuge
From the nightmare I had

I saw myself prostrate
Before the idols of infidels

But dreams are never trivial
Fate is scheming something

To know what it means
We must go to Rome'

Seven thousand devoted pupils
Donning cloaks, carrying staffs

Weeping and wailing aloud
Gathered around their master

'O master of our hankering souls
Our lives are an offering to you

You showed us the right path
Why shouldn't we obey you?'

With great love and respect
They followed him to Rome

They roamed streets and bazaars
Following closely his each step

A gorgeous mansion caught his eye
In it he spotted a wondrous beauty

Sitting at the window alone
Fully absorbed in herself

Combing her lustrous locks
Baring her dizzying head

Doing her beautiful hair
As if lashing coiling serpents

Flaunting black hyacinth curls
Threading roses in wreaths

A vermilion mark on her forehead
Whose redness was beyond compare

A black dot in that mark
A brand on the tulip's heart

Eyelashes pointed like swords
Killing lions with her glances

A mole between her eyebrows
A crow in the midst of flight

Eyebrows bent like arched bows
Shooting a shower of arrows

Her eyes did all the talking
And watched lovers falling

One could ask those eyelashes
'Who could bear those darts?'

Her mouth opened like a bud
And brows bent like bows

Her eyes were languid with drinking
Perhaps from the wine cups of gnosis

The kohl-rimmed eyes were magical
A single glance smote the Sheikh

One look at the Hindu girl
And her viper locks stung him

Her crystal-clear bosom
Outshone the Aleppo mirror

Beauty and love surged in tandem
Sheikh San'ān swooned and fell

The intoxicating beauty of the girl
Robbed him of all his senses

When the Hindu girl cast a look
Sheikh San'ān was blown away

He fainted under her window
Men came rushing from all sides

His pupils started raising wails
'O our revered master!

O leader of the chosen ones
Famous in Rome and Syria

O master, hold yourself back
Don't tug at love's rope

Do say no to the creed of love
We will cherish you in our hearts'

He said, 'O my dear pupils
And keepers of the true faith

I can't plumb the sea of love
My holy calm is turned to air

I must take the bridge of "the Apparent"[196]
To cross the tumultuous river of love

Deep has she stabbed me
What inexorable necessity!

Love's flame now licks my heart
Tell me, how should I deal with it?'

This was an unheard calamity
The Sheikh uttering blasphemy

They resigned him to God
And returned to Mecca

He stayed there for a while
With eyes riveted on her

Then the Hindu girl called out
'O leader of the Muslims

What has held you spellbound?
Thrown you into the dust of disgrace

Renouncing peace and comfort
You embrace sorrow and pain!

Ask for alms and I'll give you
My hands will reach out to you

A bowl of gold coins, if you wish
But don't throw away your staff'

He said, 'Alms are not what I want
Read the meaning behind my wailing

Since you've shown up
I tarry here bewildered

I saw your rosy cheeks and now
They are engraved on my heart

Whom should I relate my pain to?
These eyes have left me mesmerized

Regard my woeful state
I am sick, no, dead!

How drunk are your eyes!
Your fiery looks kill me

My dear moon-faced sweetheart
I am burning in love's fire

You have caught me unawares
God knows where I am heading

Trapped by your mole and curls
I am like a wild struggling deer

How rosy are your lips?
Not to be had on the market

Your teeth—pearls strung on a thread
Sucking life out of forlorn lovers

Now that my piety is gone
Come, let us be friends'

The Hindu girl spoke up then
'Sheikh, rein in your passion

Old man, be gone from here
We are an ill-matched pair

Why are you waiting at my door?
Gold and brass don't mix well

O crazy love-besotted Sheikh
Where have you come from?

I have my kith and kin
They will take this ill

My fame spreads far and wide
I will become a butt of ridicule

If my enemies catch a whiff
They will start spying on me

You will be killed disgracefully
A sorry end for a savant'

'O Hindu girl, what's come over me?
I am bereft of all attachments

Love has put me to shame
Shall I have to die twice?'

She said, 'Sheikh, listen carefully
Throw your scripture in the fire

Put aside your cloak and rosary
Wear a girdle, chant my idol's name

Renounce the faith of Islam
And I'll shower you with favours

Turn away from your faith
I'll cherish you in my bosom

Love's poison will consume you
And my dower is a million coins

O Sheikh, crazy, weary and wretched
You are too poor to be my groom

If your passion does not wane
Come and be my swineherd

If you mingle with my pigs
You will surely have me'

'O Hindu girl, wait a while
I will obey your command

Mighty love has made me helpless
Say yes and I'll pay your dower

If wealth is what you want
I'll send a word to my friends

Though they are far away
And I have no one except God

I will surely do your bidding
And stay where you want me

Look once into my wistful eyes
Thereafter I will rejoice forever

Reveal to me your secrets
Who has chiselled your figure?

Who has taught you speech?
And made your silvery hands?

Who gave you a sunny face?
Are His treasures exhausted?

Radiant is your forehead
A moon shining from afar

Your nose is like *alif* in Allah
An image engraved on bone china

Your upright, immaculate figure
Bears no sign of fatigue or sorrow

Who gave you such brightness?
And this heart-ravishing mole?'

The lover was honest and truthful
And lost utterly in the beloved

His heart knew nothing but love
His body refused food and drink

~

Song

'At your bidding Sheikh San'ān renounced his piety
O Hindu girl, my bewitching love, give ear to my wails!

The world is a mirage, how many have wasted away!
Heal my pain, be pleased with me, my love is very deep
Don't put on airs, all lives will end on a shriek of mourning
O Hindu girl, my bewitching love, give ear to my wails!

The Great Fashioner has crafted you like a beautiful doll
Stay awhile and save the Sheikh's heart from
crumbling down
O Heaven's doll, my dark abode is lit up by the lustre
of your visage
O Hindu girl, my bewitching love, give ear to my wails!

Who has braided your tresses? O my love without a
down!
Give up this swinging gait; come, drain the cups of wine
To be friends with you I have deserted my country
O Hindu girl, my bewitching love, give ear to my wails!

Be with me now; let the parrot meet the wild mynah
Neither I nor you can escape the claws of death
Your black curls and silvery earlobes are worthy of pearls
O Hindu girl, my bewitching love, give ear to my wails!

Once with you, all my maladies will be cured
Candles melt yearning for you

And the kingly box tree sheds off disease
How much more will I endure this parting?
Your black viper tresses have coiled around my neck
O Hindu girl, my bewitching love, give ear to my wails!

You have demolished my delicate body
Now redeem a desolate me
Your beauty has left me tottering, I have lost my footing.
Under the open sky I bared my body to the crescent
and stars
O Hindu girl, my bewitching love, give ear to my wails!

You have slain me, now don't let my life
be a burden on you. You tease me still
Now grab me, tossing your hyacinth curls
O love without mercy!
O Hindu girl, my bewitching love, give ear to my wails!

In a sudden flash you showed your lustrous cheeks
I stole a glimpse of your face through the black tresses
scattered on it
Hear my single prayer and my wounds will heal
O Hindu girl, my bewitching love, give ear to my wails!

Drops of dew glistening on your tulip face
And eyebrows arching like bows
Pray, shoot an arrow from them
Stab me with your dagger-shaped nose
And bruise my heart with your neck
O Hindu girl, my bewitching love, give ear to my wails!

Many are ruffled by your vermilion mark and many
are burning still
Hearing of you, the god Indra has lost all sleep
Alive for your sake alone, the crimson rose blooms
O Hindu girl, my bewitching love, give ear to my wails!

I will go now and serve hermits and yogis
I know nothing helps when love grips a man tight
O Hindu girl, my bewitching love, give ear to my wails!'

~

Just then the girl gave out a shriek
'Your words have ignited my bones

O Sheikh of great eloquence
Your words are a magical spell

I was a girl of great fame
Bewitching, proud, hidden

But your love has floored me
Layla has fallen for Majnun

I have tested your devotion
Oh, I pledge my life to you!'

~

The Sheikh's pupils took to solitude
Pondering over his misery ruefully

Till one night one of them had a dream
In which he saw the holy Prophet himself

All pupils begged him to intercede
On behalf of their wretched master

'O Prophet, our sorrow is great
Grant us our passionate prayer

Our master, the great San'ān
Is enamoured of an infidel girl

He has renounced the faith of Islam
His love has brought him disgrace

We, his pupils, are perplexed
Will our master burn in hell?

He was a man of stout heart
Pray, bring him back to faith'

The Prophet listened, then said
'A man like San'ān is not lost

He is perfect in knowledge
And peerless in humility

Though he's fallen to beauty's charms
And flung away his sense and piety

Divine grace has favoured him
He is now privy to love's mystery

He has witnessed the Truth unveil
And accomplished a rare feat

By exploring the "Garden of Attributes"
He has fathomed the meaning of the "Essence"[197]

He has negated his egoistic self
And set aside his conceit and ken

Don't think he's debased
He has gained in vision

Rejoice you, all his friends
God covers up all infirmities'

Sheikh Attār had this dream
He revealed it to his friends

Friends gave thanks to the Almighty
Sheikh San'ān would be redeemed

Pouring tears of blood
They ran to their master

They traced him to his place
And found him in a pitiable state

Worn out by endless waiting
His body smeared with ash

No cloak he wore or crown
Only begged her importunately

'O man, turn sincerely to your Lord
And humble yourself before Him'

Attār has a profound remark:
'Love and unfaith are contraries'[198]

Friends gave out a deafening cry
'Behold the torments of love

What has come over you, our Sheikh?
What have you gained through this?

You who occupied a high station
Your faith was as firm as seeing

Once the sun of the true faith
Now a deserter of *qibla* and the Kāba!

What is the object of your obeisance?
Arched eyebrows of an infidel girl?

O you, who were rapt in devotion
Who has torn away your rosary?

Who led you to this place?
Who made you wear a girdle?

The head that bowed in *namāz*
Should bow again in Mecca.'

~

'Friends, don't ask me anything
I sigh, I burn, I suffer!

This grinding journey of love
Has brought me ignominy

For a glimpse of her lovely face
And a waft of her fragrant curls

The Hindu girl gave me one look
And I outsoared Heaven's throne

She combed her lovely tresses
And I became a lover in frenzy

Having delved deep into the sea of love
I am freed from both faith and unfaith[199]

I have plumbed the bottom of that sea
And gathered pearls and corals

What place have I come to?
Is it the Kāba or Rome?

In her cheeks and eyebrows
I have seen the Truth manifest

I bore with the unbearable
And got rid of all doubts

I reached the station of "two bow-lengths"[200]
And attained a faith like seeing

The more I desired that wondrous face
The more I bid farewell to cold reason

Let reason be renamed as slave
And love rechristened as God

"Right" and "wrong" occupy reason
While love suspends all judgement

The slaves of reason lick the dust
Myriad are love's silken robes

Love can teach numerous lessons
Layla is one lesson, Majnun another

I am a reveller in the tavern
Not a name-chanting Sheikh

That which I used to deny outright
I have come to affirm now

For long I trod the path of piety[201]
Such grace is not found there

Those lit up by love's radiance
Know well the Sheikh's ordeal'

The pupils raised a clamour
'O our mentor, our father!

This is what the dream meant
O master, let us go to the Kāba'

Each talked to him in private
And persuaded him to come

The news travelled to the Hindu girl
Her heart felt a love for Islam

That veiled bewitching narcissus
With two hyacinths tied to her sides[202]

Came running after the Sheikh
Smitten deeply with his love

She who used to make wine
And pour it into cups

Broke the idol in the idol house
And smashed all the wine cups

Overwhelmed by love's power
She submitted to the Sheikh

'I am leaving my country
To be with you forever

I have renounced disbelief
And burnt my sacred thread

I have deserted my kinsmen
And accepted your true faith

My parents who rule over Rome
I have given up on them too

I offer you my remaining life
And care nothing of infamy

Hope brings me to you
Stand by me now

Look straight into my eyes
I am consumed by your love

Divorce your grief and anger
I offer myself to you now

I do not ask of you your wealth
Just be with me everywhere

Reveller, you drive me crazy
Let the two lovers make merry'

'O Hindu girl, what do you desire?
The love you ask for is alien to me

What for are your blandishments?
Stop, your beguilement is in vain

Why do you deck your locks?
Appearance no longer lures me

Don't exult in glamour and riches
Don't flaunt your mole and tresses

Lay off pride and envy
Cleanse your heart of rust

Abjure your ego and self-love
You will realize your essence'

'My selfhood has vanished
Command me and I will obey'

He gave her some crucial lessons
She proclaimed the *kalimah*[203]

'Strive for that which is worthy
Adam's form is a mere sketch

Form flickers and peters out
Form is a slave to the essence

Think not of life as a trifle
Cleanse yourself of all dross

Your ego is an impediment
Don't stumble, get over it'

Twice she uttered God's holy name
And surrendered her soul to Him

Remember this each day
Dying so is a blessing

She attained the union fast
And died a saint's death

Mahmud Gāmi has no more to say
This was Sheikh Sanʿān's tale

5. Mansur Nāmah

Mansur's Tale

Praise be to God, the Self-sufficient One
Who neither begets nor is begotten

Then countless blessings on the Prophet
Listen to this story of an eminent man

Mansur Hallāj was a resident of Baghdad
The crown of the men of love and gnosis

He observed the law for fifty years
And then got fully immersed in God

Within and without, he became one with God
'I am God, I am God,' he began to chant

A drop fell into the sea of Oneness
The sea indeed lives inside the drop

He began to reveal secrets recklessly
The news was carried to the king

'Sheikh Mansur is an apostate now
He is saying, "I am He, I am He"

The law prescribes execution for him
From the gallows throw him into fire'

The king said, 'I will admonish him
How can I order Mansur's death?

He is panacea for my sorrows and pain
How can I order the killing of a saint?'

Mansur got engrossed completely in God
A drop mingled in the sea doesn't turn back

Defying the king, the mindless mob went after
Mansur
'They are like blind men,' says a verse in the
Scripture[204]

A multitude gathered on all sides
The innocent man was dragged to Idgāh

'I am God, I am God,' he started again
Suddenly everybody looked like Mansur

He stood out from the vulgar crowd
They realized he was a man of God

Disgraced, they returned to their homes
After a few days, Mansur set out again

He found a parrot fallen dead
Quickened it, and it flew away

Now he became a fairy, uttering 'I am He'
Now a young boy shining like the moon

In every form he said, 'I am the Truth'
Streets were filled with swelling crowds

To proclaim this, he assumed different shapes
Courting infamy and the multitudes' scorn

Some among men fell on his feet
Revering him and seeking his blessings

While some wanted to hunt him down
To catch and send him to the prison

But none had the power to do so
He escaped them like light or wind

Mansur himself walked into the prison
He entered the cell cheerfully

He asked four hundred prisoners to come out
At his command all walked out free, fearlessly

When the jailer saw Mansur's stature
He offered his allegiance to him

In the prison he again said, 'I am the Truth'
His words were carried to the scholars

Mansur stayed inside the prison for sometime
Now praying, now saying, 'I am the Truth'

They put shackles around his neck
And fettered his hands and feet

'Whom do you worship, if you are He?'
'To nobody but myself I offer immolation'

When judges ordered he be put to death
Mansur disappeared from the prison

Saying 'no one', he would efface himself
Saying 'except God', he would reappear[205]

In the prison Mansur prayed passionately
Offering a thousand prayers every day

People decided to complain to the king
'Mansur is corrupting people's faith

For the sake of the Prophet's creed
Mansur must be sentenced to death'

Two savants, Shibli and Sayyid sensed
An imminent danger to Mansur's life

Junayd went to the prison to see him
His tongue chanting, 'I am the Truth'

Junayd said, 'Mansur, you are deranged
You have disregarded the lesson of love

Our master and crowning glory is Muhammad
Even he is barred from being so explicit'

Mansur said, 'Stop disputing with me on this
I have reached a station inaccessible to you

The self is an impediment in the path to Oneness
The secret of Oneness is still hidden from you'

Junayd left the prison in utter frustration
'Mansur will stain the earth with his blood'

Shibli then pleaded with Mansur
'Desist, stick to the trodden path'

Mansur replied, 'Don't irk me much
Once and for all, I am absorbed in Him

I beheld the Beloved's visage without a veil
My mind and body are plunged in that spectacle

I am not Mansur, I am He Himself
My entire being is one with Him'

He revealed the great secret to Shibli
Who bade him a tearful farewell'

Finally, an intimate friend came from Isfahān
Known as the 'Great Master' throughout the world

He went straight to Mansur's prison
'Why did you disclose the great secret?'

He replied, 'I got absorbed in the sea of Truth
Indeed, it is He who taught me this lesson

O Great Master, do me one favour
Tell them this man should be killed'

'How can I do that?' disputed the Sheikh
'How can I ask for an innocent life?

You animate the world with your breath
Men of gnosis are wonderstruck by you

You have infused a new life into them
They are now drunk on the wine of gnosis

"They are living, not dead," you read avidly[206]
Thus, you came to be the crown of the martyrs

You put on the mantle of self-abnegation
And attained the status of "living with God"

Absorbed in the divine, you became light
His essence became manifest through you'

The Great Master then left Mansur
Taking the jailed saint's word to the people:

'Will you be pleased if I am crucified?
Will you be pleased if I am thrown into fire?

Though fire burns up the ardent moth
He beholds his beloved in its midst'

The men of learning went to the king
'Mansur is creating chaos in the land

People follow him and abjure their faith
If he is not executed, Islam will perish'

The king consulted Junayd on the matter
'Is Mansur punishable with death?'

Junayd, the learned one, issued an edict
'He must die, says the supreme jurist'

The unruly mob took him to the gibbet
The ardent lovers wept bitterly for him

He desired the decree of death for himself
And graced the gibbet with his presence

As they tied his hands and feet tight
The ropes were coming apart in threads

Seeing this, Shibli wept hard and long
'Why did you bring this upon yourself?

The secret of the union evaded you
You fell away from the Prophet's path'

Mansur cried out from the gibbet
'O heedless, scheming, faithless people

You know nothing of your own faith
I am Ahmad with *meem* expunged'[207]

For a while he kept mocking the ascetics
Then as a wave he was immersed in the sea

Suddenly Mansur disappeared from the gibbet
Throwing some truth lovers into deep ecstasy

Ascetics and the riff-raff were struck dumb
Now he appeared below, now in the sky

For a time, he remained hidden from all eyes
Some say for six months, some more than that

After six months he reappeared on the gibbet
More restless than ever for the divine union

From the gibbet he shouted, 'I am the Truth'
The lover and the beloved were closer than ever

Again, he cried, 'I am the Truth,' loud and clear
Hearing this, all those present lost their senses

Everybody started saying, 'I am the Truth'
Soon the *jinn*, birds and animals joined in[208]

The third time he cried, 'I am the Truth'
Those enraptured regained their senses

They cut off his limbs, he bled profusely
He started doing ablutions with his blood

Shibli asked, 'What is this you are doing?'
'This is lovers' ablution,' was his reply

'Ablution from blood befits me today
Hail him who attains this highest station'

As Mansur's blood fell on the ground
It inscribed the word 'Allah' everywhere

And as it flowed down the streets
It kept saying, 'I am God, I am God'

Stones pelted from all sides and crushed his bones
But every hair stood up saying, 'I am God'

A friend picked a flower and threw at him
He cried, 'Your flower has hurt me more[209]

Their battering stones feel like flowers to me
You will know it when you know the truth'

Then they severed off his head on the gibbet
He cried, 'Love, you have trammelled my being'

Finally, they set him ablaze in a raging fire
The fire died out, the lover met his Beloved

The wind carried his ashes into the sea
Witnessing this, the people were baffled

Now the sea started chanting the words
'I am God, I am God, I am God'

To the chagrin of his ignorant detractors
His image appeared on the surface of water

Like a cauldron on boil or the trumpet's blast
Great effulgence arose from the sea that day

True lovers discerned what he achieved
The drop had attained union with the sea

How can you fathom his august state?
Learn that only God knows the best

Jāmi has related this story long ago
Gāmi relates it again in Kashmiri

For the sake of that great saint, my Lord
Fill Mahmud's breast with pure love!

～

6. Pahael Nāmah

The Shepherd's Tale

Moosa saw a shepherd trudging along
Chanting aloud: 'O my lovable God!'[210]

Crying, wailing, raising lamentations
As if telling God his tale of woe

Tears unstoppable flowed from his eyes
'Where are you, my Lord?' he kept saying

His woe-stricken heart knew no comfort
'May my life be yours, listen to me

Let my dearest ones be sacrificed for you
Yearning for you, my moon has eclipsed

O Lord, I offer you my body and soul
My parents, my children, no, my life!

O Lord, I pine for a glimpse of yours!
Each fibre of my being is consumed by love

I wish my head could fall on your feet
I will be obliged if you appear to me

For You, I have lost my sleep
My body refuses to eat or drink

O Lord, if I see you alone somewhere
I will lap you up into my eyes

If I saw you, I would become your slave
Circle around you and get rid of grief

I reared my sheep and goats for you
If you eat from them, I shall be blessed

I am besotted with your love, hear me
Come once and be with me for a while

You have cast a spell on me
I languish here in your wait

No one knows you axed my heart with love
Showing no pity, you hacked it to shreds

Sit by me on my porch for a while
If you can't come, show up in a dream

Away from you, I smoulder from within
In search of you, I wander aimlessly

O Exalted One, could I comb your tresses!
In quest of you, clever men have turned to dust

Where are you? I search for you everywhere
I am trapped, my heart is about to burst

By the stream banks I will wait for you
Offer you cream and dress your curls

My love, why don't you reveal yourself?
You have reduced my bones to dust

My love, desire for you has torched me down
Longing has melted me like summer's snow

My love, I am a sacrifice to your holy name
To have you, I will barter my life too

Could I sacrifice my head at your feet?
My youth is spent seeking out you in vain

You have riddled my heart, do come
O beloved sans mercy, do come!

Frantically, I am looking for you everywhere
Wandering the plains and climbing the hills

If you be barefoot, I will make you sandals
Wash your clothes and clean your body

Let all my goats be slaughtered for you
O you, for whom my wails won't end!

If you fall ill, I shall nurse you to health
Serve you tirelessly like a doting slave

Keep your word, I will serve you milk and ghee
Who can match my affliction from separation?

If you be hungry, I will serve you delicacies
If you be thirsty, I will offer sweet milk

Cook for you the best of my lambs
Stitch your robes with golden threads

Say you are hungry and I will place
A hundred dishes on your table

Say you are cold and I will lull
You to sleep in my warm lap

I will stitch you clothes, pick your lice
Offer you the milk of my best goats

Feed you cheese, bread and butter
And offer you the best of dates

If your feet are dirty, I will wash them
And wait on you to do your bidding

If I could find a way to your home
I would run errands all day for you

With fragrant musk I would oil your curls
I am a lover in the grip of your charm'

When Moosa heard the shepherd's song
He stood dumbstruck, then addressed him

'Shepherd, who is that you are speaking to?
Who is the lover whose love you profess?'

'I speak to Him who created me from nothing
Hides Himself and makes me search for Him

I speak to Him who created the throne
Who has put a raging fire in my breast

He who brought Heavens into existence
He who has fettered my neck and feet

He whose spark animates my soul
He whose love has left me in ruins

He for whom I am utterly devastated
Who has made off with my gashed heart'

Moosa said: 'Alas, you are undone!
Your faith is wrecked, you are damned

If you don't stop uttering these abominations
A heavenly blast will destroy all creation

O shepherd, why do you speak blasphemy?
Better you stitched your profane lips

Who will you feed, wash and offer drink?
Who will feel cold and you lull to sleep?

O foolish shepherd, He is above such wants
Eating, drinking, bearing and being born'

With these words Moosa jilted him harshly
The woe-stricken one became even more so

He said: 'Moosa, you have stitched my lips
Your rebuke has torched by anguished soul'

He tore his shirt and drew a long sigh
And in no time took to his heels

He abandoned his herd and went far away
And started wailing even more than before

No sooner had he deserted his herd
Than the Almighty spoke to Moosa[211]

A voice from above fell into his ears:
'You have severed my servant from Me

Were you sent to join men to me?
Or to drive them away from Me?

What is this you have done?
My lover is now torn from Me

My lovers know my love's sweetness
An afflicted heart knows no manners

What is blame to you is praise to him
What is poison to you is honey to him

What is fire to you is light to him
What is thorn to you is rose to him

I care not for what meets the eye
I only care for what lies within

If love's warmth animates his heart
I care not for the roughness of his word

The martyr's blood is not a thing to wash away
A hundred good acts are not worth his folly

Don't seek guidance from the drunk[212]
Never ask them to darn their rags

The creed of love is different from all others
God's lovers are beyond faith and sects

What do I need your prayer and fasting for?
I want a heart aflame with love's fervour'

God's words made Moosa wiser
He became privy to the hidden truth

God revealed to him many more secrets
Those which the tongue can scarcely utter

As they fell into Moosa's ear
His seeing and hearing fell together

God's reprimand illumined his eyes
He rushed back looking for the shepherd

He found him at a distant place
Forlorn, exhausted and distraught

Humbly, Moosa began: 'My dear one
Your anguished heart is dear to your Lord

Your heart's bane has turned into a boon
Your blasphemy has fetched a very high price

So, keep saying what you said before
The good God says he is pleased with you

Care not for manners and protocols
Say fearlessly what your heart holds'

'Woe to me, if I have annoyed God
Your words have made me forget my wails

I am at a higher station than before
Your whip has made my stallion run fast

You cracked the whip of love on me
I am effaced into God's grandeur

May I ever remain in this rapture divine!
May you ever flourish and be blessed!'[213]

'Long live, O love, our sweet frenzy!
O you, the cure of all our ills![214]

Cure of our pride and self-love
O you, our Plato and Galen!

The mould of dust rises to heaven through love
Mountains start dancing and gain vision

Love infused life into the Mount Sinai
Sinai got drunk and Moosa fell unconscious[215]

Love holds the boundless skies together
Love comprehends the vastness of the earth

Love is the flame which consumes the dry and wet
Love is the fire that melts the mighty Sinai

Love throws the wise into frenzy
Love is a blessing for the living hearts

Love puts the skies into motion
Love refreshes the entire Universe

Love is the mirror of God's light
Love severs you from all except Him

Lord, let me taste the fruit of love
How long will I wait for its burning touch?'

Notes

Introduction

1. Quoted by Abdul Ahad Āzād, *Kashmiri Zabān aur Shāyri*, Vol. 2 (Srinagar: Jammu and Kashmir Academy of Art, Culture and Languages, 2005), p. 283.

2. There is no study on Gāmi available in English, except a short monograph titled *Mahmud Gami* (1991) by Muzaffar Azim in the Sahitya Academy series 'Makers of Indian Literature'. In Kashmiri, too, there is scant critical writing available on him.

3. Āzād mentions a few of these anecdotes. According to one, Gāmi suddenly started writing verse when his son Shah Sultan died at a young age. A poem found in his *divan* beginning with 'My life be yours, yours, yours, My dear Shah Sultan' is invoked to substantiate this claim. Another story tells of a wandering mystic who arrived in Gāmi's village and asked him to draw a puff from a hookah, which he did and fainted. One regaining his senses, he began to utter poetry.

4. This poem is quoted by Ghulam Muhammad Shād in 'Mahmud Gāmi sund nāyāb kalām te amyich ahmiyat',

in *Anhār: A Special Issue on Mahmud Gāmi*, ed. Qazi Zahoor (Srinagar: Department of Kashmiri, University of Kashmir, 1990), pp. 52–79.

5. A hyperbolic expression not to be taken literally.

6. A famous ancient king of Persia.

7. According to the Hijra calendar.

8. According to Muzaffar Azim, 'Burkhardt complains that he did not get the required help in reading the text, could not find a Kashmiri dictionary and the Pandit scholars who helped him with the text were not knowledgeable enough.' See Muzaffar Azim, 'Mahmudas paeth karne aamets tehqīqi te tanqīdi kaem', in *Anhār: A Special Issue on Mahmud Gāmi*, ed. Qazi Zahoor (1990), p. 35.

9. A reference to the Quranic Chapter 92, Verse 1, 'By the night when it covers' and Chapter 93, Verse 1, 'By the morning brightness'.

10. See *Kuliyāt Mahmud Gāmi*, ed. Naji Munawar (Srinagar: Jammu and Kashmir Academy of Art, Culture and Languages, 1977), p. 5.

11. Shafi Shauq, for example, says, 'However, in view of perfection of expression and form, her (Lal Ded's) poetry seems to be the culmination of a long poetic tradition that remains hidden to the present-day reader.' See 'Towards Understanding Lal Ded', *Sheeraza*, Vol. 15, No. 4 (October–December 2019), p. 16.

12. See Āzād, *Kashmiri Zabān aur Shāyri*, Vol. 2, p. 299. Rudaki (858–941) is widely regarded as the first great literary genius of the modern Persian and a founder of classical Persian literature. Chaucer's (1343–1400) place in the English poetic tradition is well known.

13. Shafi Shauq, 'Mahmudun Shayrāna Maqām', in *Anhār: A Special Issue on Mahmud Gāmi*, ed. Qazi Zahoor (Srinagar: Department of Kashmiri, University of Kashmir, 1990), p. 88.

14. Rahmān Rāhi endorses Shauq's estimate in 'Mahmud Gamiyun Ghazal', in *Anhār: A Special Issue on the Art of the Ghazal*, ed. Qazi Zahoor (2004), p. 68. Another critic, Professor Ghulam Muhammad Shād describes Gāmi as the source for the poetry of Rasul Mir, Maqbool Shah Krālwari, Abdul Ahad Nāzim and others. In style, imagery and content, he calls the poetry of Rasul Mir and Nāzim the echoes of Gāmi. See *Anhār: A Special Issue on Mahmud Gāmi*, ed. Qazi Zahoor (1990), p. 53.

15. Quoted by M.Y. Taing in *Kuliyāt-e Rasul Mir*, ed. M.Y. Taing (Jammu and Kashmir Academy of Art, Culture and Languages, 2009), p. 26.

16. Alexander Beecroft, *An Ecology of World Literature: From Antiquity to the Present Day* (London: Verso, 2015), p. 153.

17. Ibid.

18. Ibid., p. 154.

19. Āzād repeats the point throughout volume 1 of his three-volume book. For instance, 'The undesirable trend of imitating Persian starts with Mahmud Gāmi' (p. 246); 'In my opinion it is incontrovertible that the unnecessary borrowing from other languages has damaged our language and literature immensely' (p. 43); 'By the time of Habba Khatoon, Persian culture had left a deep imprint on Kashmir. Kashmir had freed itself from the chains of Sanskrit but had now come under the hegemony of Persian' (p. 54). He regrets how this 'baneful' influence only increased from the day of Habba Khatoon down to the 19th century.

20. J.L. Kaul, 'Kashmiri Poetry: Some Forms and Themes', in *The Literary Heritage of Kashmir*, ed. K.L. Kalla (Delhi: Mittal Publications, 1985), pp. 101–02.

21. In the same essay, J.L. Kaul regrets that some writers, for instance, Master Zinda Kaul, himself a poet of

renown, have accepted the validity of terms such as 'Hindu Kashmiri' and 'Muslim Kashmiri' while introducing Parmanand's poetry, implying thereby a wide divergence in the diction and subject matter of the poets of the two communities. For J.L. Kaul, no such distinction is tenable. It is, however, to be noted, that despite significant overlaps, a difference is easily discernible in the works of the Muslim and Hindu poets if only for the reason that what is called 'secular poetry' was yet to come into existence and religion was the primary source from which poets of respective communities drew.

22. The term *Kashmiriyat* best defines this tendency. Very often *Kashmiriyat* is invoked to suggest a cultural heritage and a socio-religious ethos characterized by somewhat fluid religious identities unique to Kashmir. However, nothing in the religious or literary tradition of Kashmir validates such an idea.

23. S.H. Nasr, *Three Muslim Sages: Avicenna-Suharwardi-Ibn 'Arabi* (Delmar: Caravan Books, 1997), p. 105.

24. Ibid., p. 106.

25. See William Chittick, 'The Perfect Man as the Prototype of the Self in the Sufism of Jami', *Studia Islamica*, No. 49 (1979), pp. 135–57 (Brill).

26. J.T.B. de Bruijn, *Persian Sufi Poetry: An Introduction to the Mystical Use of Classical Persian Poems* (Surrey: Curzon Press, 1997), p. 25.

27. Ibid.

28. *Vatsun* No. 4.

29. Cyrus Ali Zargar, *Sufi Aesthetics: Beauty, Love, and the Human Form in the Writings of Ibn 'Arabi and 'Iraqi* (Columbia: University of South Carolina Press, 2013), p. 12.

30. For some Sufis there is just the difference of one letter *meem* م between احد, i.e., God, and احمد, one of the names of the Prophet Muhammad. The alphabetical symbolism invoked here suggests the idea of unity of being.

31. See the explanation below on lxv–lxvii where Mansur's proclamation 'I am the Truth' is discussed.

32. Shafi Shauq, 'Mahmud Gami: Founder of Mystic Poetry in Kashmiri', *Sheeraza: A Quarterly Journal of Culture and Literature*, Vol. 15, No. 1 (January–March 2019), p. 1.

33. Lowry Nelson, 'The Rhetoric of Ineffability: Toward a Definition of Mystical Poetry', *Comparative Literature*, Vol. 8, No. 4 (Autumn, 1956), pp. 323–36.

34. *Vatsun* No. 7.

35. *Vatsun* No. 9.

36. *Vatsun* No. 2.

37. S.H. Nasr, Foreword to *Divine Love: Islamic Literature and the Path to God* by William C. Chittick (New Haven: Yale University Press, 2013), p. vii.

38. The moth as the symbol of self-sacrifice is a well-known poetic theme. In his *Sawānih*, Muhammad Ghazali dilates upon various dimensions of the symbol. Attār in his 'Mantiqut Tayr' illustrates his idea of the three modes of knowing using the symbol of the moth. A Sufi, avers Attār, knows the meaning of fire like the moth which burns itself in it.

39. *Vatsun* No. 32.

40. *Vatsun* No. 28 (*dunya cho gam koi ghar lolo/pāne myāne ti kar sare lolo*)

41. *Vatsun* No. 99 (*aendrim dod be kas wanith zānay/ musāfir pāne myānay ho*)

42. *Vatsun* No. 69.

43. *Nazm* No. 4.

44. J.L. Kaul, 'Kashmiri Poetry: Some Forms and Themes', in *The Literary Heritage of Kashmir*, ed. K.L. Kalla (Delhi: Mittal Publications, 1985), p. 97.

45. Jonathan Culler, *Theory of the Lyric* (Cambridge: Harvard University Press, 2015), p. 21.

46. Naji Munawar and Shafi Shauq, *Kaeshir Zaban te Adabuk Tawarikh* (Srinagar: Ali Muhammad and Sons, 2014), p. 132.

47. The American New Critic J.C. Ransom wrote: 'The poet does not speak in his own but in an assumed character, not in the actual but in an assumed situation, and the first thing we do as readers of poetry is to determine precisely what character and what situation are assumed. In this examination lies the possibility of critical understanding and, at the same time, of the illusion and the enjoyment.' *The World's Body* (Port Washington, New York: Kennikat Press, 1964) pp. 254–55.

48. Jonathan Culler, *Theory of the Lyric*, p. 226.

49. Victor Erlich, 'Limits of the Biographical Approach', *Comparative Literature*, Vol. 6 (1954), p. 135.

50. Paul E. Losensky, *Welcoming Fighani: Imitation and Poetic Individuality in the Safavid–Mughal Ghazal* (Costa Mesa, California: Mazda Publishers, 1998), p. 56.

51. T. Raina, *A History of Kashmiri Literature* (New Delhi: Sahitya Academy, 2002), p. 41. Raina contrasts, erroneously in my opinion, what he calls 'the single mood' of the *vatsun* with the changing ones of the *ghazal*. Muzaffar Azim, on the other hand, ably discusses the shift of mood in the *vatsun*. See his *Mahmud Gami*, p. 18.

52. Abdul Ahad Āzād, *Kashmiri Zabān aur Shāyri*, (Srinagar: Jammu and Kashmir Academy of Art,

Culture and Languages, 2005) regrettably, conflates the two throughout his study.

53. Rahmān Rāhi has drawn attention to Gāmi's *ghazals* and demonstrated how they actually are much closer to the *vatsun* form. Rāhi also suggests that some of Gāmi's poems cannot be classified either as *ghazals* or *vatsuns* because they evince characteristics of both and constitute a separate category. See Rahmān Rāhi's essay 'Mahmud Gamiyun Ghazal', in *Anhār: A Special Issue on the Art of the Ghazal*, ed. Qazi Zahoor (Srinagar: Department of Kashmiri, University of Kashmir, 2004), pp. 67–80.

54. This claim has been disputed by critics such as M.Y. Taing and Muzaffar Azim, both of whom state that Momin Saeb's 'Mantiqut Tayr' was the first masnavi written in Kashmiri. See M.Y. Taing's *'Kaeshir shāyri parkhāvnuk byākh andāz'*, p. 7, foreword to *Kaeshir Sufi Shayri*, ed. Moti Lal Saqi (Srinagar: Jammu and Kashmir Academy of Art, Culture and Languages, 1985) and Muzaffar Azim, *Mahmud Gami*, p. 2. Almost all critics, however, agree that even though the *masnavi* form might have existed in Kashmiri before Gāmi, he was the first major contributor to this genre, one who put it on a firm pedestal and provided impetus to other poets. Azim writes:

> Momin's importance lies in his having written *Mantiq-ut-Tayr* in Kashmiri under the influence of Farid-ud-din Attar, a famous Persian poet. Through this work he steals historical priority over Mahmud Gami as the first *mathnavi* writer of the language, but historical priority apart, Gami is certainly the first master of the art, who contributed substantially, and enormously influenced the subsequent *mathnavi* writers.

55. Hellmut Ritter, *Über die Bildersprache Niẓāmīs* (Berlin and Leipzig: De Gruyter, 1927) p. 61.

56. Hashmat Moayyad, *Encyclopedia Iranica*, 'Farhad (1)'. See iranicaonline.org.

57. Naji Munawar and Shafi Shauq, *Kaeshir Zabān te Adabuk Tawarikh* (Srinagar: Ali Muhammad and Sons, 2014), pp. 155, 221.

58. Shahab Ahmed notes in this regard: 'In Jāmī's poem, Zulaykhā is transformed from the agent of sinful temptation (the dominant evaluation of her in the genre of Qur'ān commentary) to the embodiment of the passion of true love (and thus a model for the Sufi love of God).' *What Is Islam* (New Jersey: Princeton University Press, 2015), p. 305.

59. In his excellent work on the romance titled *Layli and Majnun*, Ali Asghar Seyed-Gohrab writes about its popularity (Ali Asghar Seyed-Gohrab, *Layli and Majnun: Love, Madness and Mystic Longing in Nizami's Epic Romance* [Leiden: Brill, 2003], p. 27):
    This romance has proved to be one of the most imitated love stories in the vast Islamic world, especially in those countries in which Persian culture has been cultivated from the twelfth century onwards. The poem was popular among people from the Malay Peninsula to India, Turkey and Africa. Naturally there are a great number of imitations of this poem in the various languages spoken by Muslims.

60. Lalita Sinha, in her study of Layla Majnun romance, explains how the nature of the man–woman relationship in mystical poetry often involves the 'breach or infringement of usual social norms and standards of decorum of a community' (p. 42). For her, Majnun's act exemplifies the idea of 'love that knows no laws' (Ibid.). *Unveiling the Garden of Love: Mystical Symbolism in Layla Majnun and Gita Govinda* (Indiana: World Wisdom, Inc., 2008).

61. Ali Asghar Seyed-Gohrab comments on Udhrite poetry (*Layli and Majnun*, pp. 63–4):

> Udhrite love is a literary and philosophical theme, inspired by Platonic love. The prototype of Udhrite love poetry and stories goes back to pre-Islamic times . . . ' Udhrite poets used religious phraseology and allusions to idealise the female beloved. However, the Islamic influence should not be overestimated, because there are few Koranic references in this type of poetry. The use of religious vocabulary became increasingly marked with the emergence of Sufism, which borrowed several elements from Udhrism. The character-traits of the Udhrite lover, such as chastity, humble devotion, isolation, love-madness and martyrdom, were regarded by Sufis as praiseworthy qualities inevitably associated with their pure love for the divine beloved. Not only did mystics utilise short anecdotes about Udhrite lovers, particularly Layli and Majnun, to show their own relationship to the Beloved, they also took over erotic elements to be found in Udhrite poetry. From the beginning of the twelfth century, mystics employed increasingly erotic vocabulary to describe their love towards the Divine.

62. Cyrus Ali Zargar has dwelt on this motif in his *Sufi Aesthetics: Beauty, Love, and the Human Form in the Writings of Ibn 'Arabi and 'Iraqi*. He cites a few more stories, found in the Islamic hagiographical tradition, which underscore the same idea of profane love leading to the divine. Ibn Arabi's recounting of Ruzbihan Baqli's falling in love for a singing girl is patterned on the same theme. See p. 65 of the book.

63. *Guft aan yār k'az-u gasht sar-e dār buland / jormash in bud ki asrār hoveydā mikard.* He said, 'That

friend for whom the noose was raised/His crime was giving secret truths away.' Muhammad Iqbal (1877–1938) who began as a fierce critic of Mansur was convinced later that his *anal haq* meant 'the Infinite entering into the loving embrace of the finite.' Those who have defended Mansur's proclamation stress on a vital distinction between incarnation (*hulūl*), commingling (*imtizāj*) and *istighrāq* (absorption/immersion). Hujwiri, the author of the famous Sufi treatise *Kashful Mahjūb* denies that Mansur taught blasphemous ideas such as transmigration of the souls (*naskh-e arvāh*), commingling or incarnation.

64. S.H. Nasr, *Three Muslim Sages*. pp. 86–7.

65. *Medieval Romances across European Borders*, ed. Miriam Edlich-Muth (Turnhout: Brepols Publishers, 2018), p. 8.

66. Vinay Dharwadker makes the following insightful observation on the idea of secularism in the modern period (*Kabir: The Weaver's Songs* [New Delhi: Penguin Books, 2003], p. lxvii):

   In the modern period, we have come to view secularism as historically and conceptually possessing four basic orientations: (a) *a non-religious* disposition, in which secularists attempt to construct social principles and to deal with civil and civic matters by stepping outside the domain of religion altogether; (b) an *a-religious* orientation, in which secularists adopt an attitude of indifference to religion, and develop pragmatic strategies that ignore the division between the religious and the non-religious; (c) an *anti-religious* orientation, in which secularists explicitly oppose religion and seek to dismantle its institutions and structures; and (d) a *post-religious* disposition, in which secularists treat religion as a phenomenon of and in the past, and hence only of historical interest.

Needless to say, all the four orientations would have appeared quite alien to Gāmi and his contemporaries.

67. In exceptional cases, however, the poets of the period did address contemporary political and social issues. As an example, Hamidullah Shāhābādi wrote *Bibuj Nāmah* in Persian, which highlights the plight of the Kashmiris living under political oppression. In Kashmiri, Maqbool Shah Krālwari wrote *Grīs Nāmah* (The Peasant's Tale), which is a satire on the Kashmiri peasantry.

68. Quoted and translated by Jonathan Culler, 'L' *Hyberbole et l' apostrophe*: Baudelaire and the Theory of the Lyric', *Yale French Studies*, No. 125/126 (2014), pp. 85–101.

69. *Rahmate haq bar Nizāmi shud nasīb/ chus naba Mahmud Gāmi ham qarīb*
    shār vanun moakhte stanbun zāntan/yā dilo jān chuy karun birun zi tan
    These lines occur towards the end of Gāmi's *masnavi*, 'Qisae Haroon Rashid' in the 1977 edition, p. 276.

Vatsuns

1. The first poem is a typical lōl vatsun (love lyric) in which the speaker is a female addressing her friend in the beginning but immediately shifting her address to an absent lover.

2. The beloved is sometimes addressed by this epithet in Kashmiri poetry.

3. This *vatsun*, too, celebrates earthly love. The speaker is addressing her lover who has abandoned her. A pensive mood pervades the poem.

4. A mystical poem dealing with the idea of the One manifesting itself in multiplicity.

5. The mystical idea of 'unity of being'. See Introduction, p. xxvi. Cyrus Ali Zargar makes the following useful comment, 'witnessing and love result from one omnipresent reality: existence itself. This oneness is real and all-inclusive, to such an extent that a complete distinction between God and creation amounts to a sort of idolatry, since it posits the independent existence of that which maintains a constant state of need vis-à-vis God' (*Sufi Aesthetics*, p. 4).

6. Beyond the phenomenal world lies the single undifferentiated essence.

7. Every single object displays its unique beauty.

8. The speaker addresses the Creator, expressing gratitude for the gift of existence.

9. 'The throne of God', called *'arsh* in Arabic, symbolizes the highest station in divine hierarchy.

10. The chapter of oneness in the Quran is a short chapter which proclaims God's absolute transcendence and unity.

11. The bulbul and the rose, the lover and the beloved respectively, are oft-repeated images in the Perso–Arabic literary tradition used by Kashmiri poets.

12. See Introduction, p. xxxvi for the image of the moth and the flame.

13. The ascetic who only sees the apparent and is ignorant of the essence.

14. The Bountiful, that is, God.

15. A love lyric in which the speaker employs a range of images to describe the emotion of separation from her love.

16. One of the metaphors used for the beloved in Persian poetry is that of an archer shooting arrows of love.

17. An allusion to the divine beloved.
18. The beloved's mole is compared to a grain of black pepper which connotes dark colour and spicy hotness. An allusion to imported valuables from the Indian plains which was a common practice in Kashmir during Gāmi's time.
19. Jewels of Badakhshan were proverbially famous.
20. There is a sudden shift of address in this stanza from the third to the second person only to be reversed in the last line.
21. The garden of Sulaimān (Solomon), famous in the ancient world for its beauty. Some Kashmiri chroniclers have mentioned it as a sobriquet of the valley of Kashmir.
22. Nāgrāy is the hero of an ancient Kashmiri mythical story who was in love with Hīmāl. Here is the outline of the story: A poor Brahmin named Soda Ram has a nagging wife who has made his life miserable. Once, when Soda Ram is away from home, he finds a snake and decides to grab the opportunity to get rid of his wife. He takes the snake home in a bag and tells his wife that he has brought her a precious gift. Leaving her alone with the bag, he waits for the snake to come out and bite her. To the utter amazement of the couple, a beautiful baby boy comes out of the bag. The Brahmin and his wife feel blessed by his presence, name him Nāgrāy and bring him up as their own son. The child brings immense prosperity and happiness to them.

   Nāgrāy grows into a young handsome man. One day he desires to bathe in a spring. The only spring his foster-father can think of is securely fortified with high walls and belongs to a princess named Hīmāl. Nāgrāy turns into a snake, creeps through a hole in the wall, takes a dip in the spring and returns without being observed. Noticing that someone has used her spring, the princess lies in wait to catch the intruder. Nāgrāy comes to bathe again. A single glimpse at Nāgrāy strikes her deep and she immediately falls in love with him. She proposes to him and the two get married.

But Nāgrāy is no ordinary mortal. He is a serpent (nāga) from the underworld and has left pining wives behind him. When the snake-wives learn about his marriage to a human princess, they decide to reclaim their husband. Hīmāl is approached and told that her husband belongs to a low caste. As a test, she should ask him to take a dip in a spring of milk. Only if he sinks in it can he be a pure Brahmin. When asked by Hīmāl to go through the trial, Nāgrāy refuses first but yields before her stubbornness. He steps into the spring of milk, but once in it, his snake-wives start pulling him down. His repeated appeals to Hīmāl to pull him out bear no result till he is completely drowned in the spring. Terrified, Hīmāl clutches at his hair but is left only with a tuft of hair in her hand as Nāgrāy disappears into the underworld.

Thereafter, Hīmāl regrets her act and bitterly grieves her loss. An old man tells her that he has seen a serpent emerging from a spring and assuming the human form. This raises her hopes and she waits for the serpent to come out next time. Finally, a serpent does emerge and turn into a human—and lo, it is Nāgrāy! Hīmāl falls to his feet and begs him to take her along. He is deeply touched by her miserable condition, turns her into a pebble and takes her with him into the underworld. Not before long his snake-wives discover the truth about Hīmāl and start tormenting her. Finally, she is killed on the false allegation of killing the nāga children. Nāgrāy is grief-stricken. Unable to cremate her, he brings her into the upper world, embalms her, places her under a tree and visits her every week.

One day as Nāgrāy comes out of the spring, he finds Hīmāl missing. He learns that a holy man gifted with rare powers has brought her to life again. Still in the form of a serpent, he approaches the sleeping Hīmāl. The holy man's son is alarmed at the presence of a snake near her and immediately kills him. Hīmāl wakes up and cremates herself on his funeral pyre.

23. For the story of Farhād and Shīrīn, see *Masnavi* 'Khusrau Shīrīn' in this volume.

24. See *Masnavi* 'Layla Majnun' p. 198 where Majnun feigns blindness to visit Layla.

25. See *Masnavi* 'Sheikh San'ān' p. 240 and Introduction, p. lx.

26. The beloved here is the divine.

27. A reference to the Quranic verse: 'When your Lord brought forth descendants from the loins of the sons of Adam, and made them witnesses against their own selves asking them: "Am I not your Lord?" They said: "Yes, we do testify."' Surah 7, verse 172.

28. Achabal and Khanabal are famous places in south Kashmir.

29. Nimrod, according to the Old Testament, was an ancient king of Mesopotamia who rebelled against God. In the Islamic tradition, he is the arch enemy of Ibrāhīm (Abraham) who claimed divinity and persecuted the believers. In poetry, Nimrod is the symbol of pride and tyranny.

30. Shaddād in the Islamic tradition was an ancient king who tried to build a Paradise-like garden on the earth as an act of defiance against God. He, however, met

with sudden death the moment he was about to enter it. Hātim Tay was an ancient king of Yemen, very popular for his generosity.

31. The names of famous places in and around the Dal Lake in Srinagar.

32. The poem expresses a desire not to have been born at all because the journey ahead is perilous and salvation is not guaranteed. The desire not to be, is not due to the sufferings of this world but the stations the soul has to pass through to attain salvation. It, however, ends on an optimistic note since 'All except God is bound to perish'.

33. Probably a veiled reference to the 'Bridge of *Sirāt*' a bridge 'thin as the hair and sharper than the sword's edge', as some traditions have it.

34. A reference to the Quranic verse: 'Everything will perish save His countenance', Surah 28, verse 88.

35. Literally, 'the secret of secrets', meaning the secret of existence.

36. An oft-repeated theme in Islamic tradition. Adam, according to the Quran, was made from clay and God breathed His own spirit into him (Surah 15, verse 29). Another exit refers to death when the spirit leaves the body.

37. The journey of the soul is as tough as the process of transmuting a base metal into a pure one through burning.

38. Hoping for salvation without preparation is compared to going to the market with an empty pocket.

39. Literally, 'Can you bear the burden of two?' The line can also be read as a veiled allusion to the burden of sins which, according to some traditions, will have to be carried by the person in the next world.

40. The end of the body is decay. The poem is didactic in reminding the reader of the imminent disintegration.

41. A well-known tradition holds that 1,24,000 messengers have been sent in different places and different times to warn the mankind.

42. A reference to *mi'rāj*, the heavenly journey of the Prophet Muhammad interpreted by some as real and others as a dream, in which he witnessed the rewards and punishments meted out to the souls in the next life.

43. The ending strikes an optimistic note as the speaker seems sure of God's all-encompassing mercy.

44. Like some other *vatsuns*, this one is addressed by a female speaker to her friends.

45. See *Masnavi* 'Yusuf Zulaykha', p. 139–141. for a description of Yusuf when he arrives in Egypt.

46. Ruma Rishi, in Kashmiri folklore, is believed to have lived a very long life.

47. See *Masnavi* 'Khusrau Shīrīn', p. 81–92 for Farhād's story.

48. The famous Yusuf (Joseph), known for his angelic beauty. After his stepbrothers conspire against him, he is brought to Egypt and sold as a slave. A courtier buys him and takes him home where his wife falls madly in love with Joseph and tries to seduce him. Joseph avoids all such misadventures but again falls victim to the conspiracy of the courtier's wife. He lands in jail for spurning her advances. But till then many more women have lost their hearts to his matchless beauty. Zulaykha belonged to the Ād tribe.

49. Probably, an allusion to Sheikh Sādi, a celebrated poet of Persian.

50. The moment when the body convulses in throes of death.

51. The wounds of love can only be healed in the life to come. As for those who have held themselves back from treading the path of love altogether, their wounds will remain unhealed.

52. The poem is permeated with a remorseful mood on account of the speaker's failure to realize the highest truth for which life had offered an opportunity.

53. The signs of the divine beloved are usually said to be everywhere. Here, the divine is said to be seated in the beholder's very eye and yet could not be picked by him/her.

54. The bulbul is the lover and the rose the beloved. The rose is short-lived but the thorn outlives it by long.

55. The bird is the soul and the cage the body.

56. One's spiritual achievements are the only real earnings.

57. The hereafter will be the time when all that was hidden and mysterious in this world will become manifest.

58. The messenger of death.

59. This poem can be called a paean to love. Here love is personified in apostrophic addresses. For a detailed discussion on Gāmi's philosophy of love, see Introduction, p. xxvi–xxxiii.

60. A mystical idea is treated here. 'The Emperor' usually denotes God.

61. According to this mystical idea, the world of appearance will reveal its real essence in the next world.

62. Gāmi refers to the Sufi idea of the word *hu*, an Arabic pronoun meaning 'He', denoting God. Since God breathed His own spirit into Adam, for many Sufis the human soul is uncreated.

63. The Essence (*zāt*) and Attributes (*sifāt*) are terms used in theological and Sufi discourses. While God can be known through His Attributes, His Essence remains beyond human comprehension. Here, Love is talked of as putting on the attire of Attributes to manifest itself.

64. See *Masnavi* 'Layla Majnun', p. 190.

65. See *Masnavi* 'Sheikh San'ān', p. 240 and Introduction, p. lx.

66. See 'The Moth's Tale', p. 43.
67. See *Masnavi* 'Mansur Nāmah', p. 262 and Introduction, p. lxiv.
68. The address shifts in this stanza from Love to the reader.
69. Deserting one's kin for the sake of love is a recurrent motif in Kashmiri love poetry, often expressed by the lovesick woman. Layla, Zulaykha and Shīrīn, all go through the experience of estrangement from their kin in the course of love.
70. The beloved is obviously drunk, but on a wine offered by a rival.
71. Dagger is a metaphor for the nose of the beloved.
72. Evaluating the beloved's worth on the market is a common expression in Kashmiri love poetry.
73. A delightful use of the word 'thirty' because the Quran, alluded to in the preceding line, is divided into thirty equal parts for facilitating recitation.
74. The term 'there' suggests eternity.
75. God is hidden and yet manifest in His creation.
76. Tel Bal is a lake near Srinagar.

Nazms

77. The moth in Sufi poetry is the symbol of self-sacrifice in the cause of love. Gāmi's poem is probably inspired by a passage in Attār's *Mantiqut Tayr* (*The Conference of the Birds*) where Attār describes three stages of the knowledge of the beloved. A moth which learns about a burning candle from a source, another one goes to witness it himself, while the third flutters around it and finally jumps into its flame. Only the third moth, Attār's allegory suggests,

knows the real meaning of love, having attained it by experience rather than report or perception. To be annihilated in and by the beloved is the final goal of the lover.

78. Tur is Mt. Sinai where according to the Quran (7:143), Moosa begged God to reveal Himself to him. God's reply was, 'By no means can you see Me. But look upon the mount; if it abides in its place, then shall you see Me.' Mount Tur instantly turned into ashes when God let a ray of His fall on it and Moosa fell unconscious.

79. A reference to the Quranic verse 50:16: 'And indeed We have created man, and We know what suggestions his soul makes to him; for We are nearer to him than his jugular vein.'

80. A Quranic verse says: 'He is with you wherever you be'.

81. The company of those who have experienced a spiritual awakening through love is often emphasized in Sufism.

82. A tradition often quoted by Sufis.

83. See Introduction, p. xxxvii.

84. Contemplation (*fikr*) and remembrance (*zikr*) are the two equally important pillars on which a seeker has to raise his/her spiritual edifice.

85. The heedless man is one who lives an unexamined life and is absorbed in the mundane and the immediate. The pedant is deluded by bookish lore and is deprived of the direct experience of the lover.

86. A common theme in Sufi poetry is the contrast between the dry asceticism of an ascetic and the ardour and passionate longing of a true lover. Love's torment is a source of joy for the true lover.

87. The lover is God Himself whose act of creation was an act of love by which He created all humans. His blowing first into the water brought the bubble into

existence and blowing again made it lose its individual existence.

88. The close proximity of the Prophet Muhammad with God is a recurrent theme in Sufi poetry. Gāmi explains this idea in this poem and elsewhere through various images.

89. In the Sufi metaphysics, God is both transcendental and immanent. The Prophet's nearness to God is suggested through the complex image of a boat in the water with some water in it. In turn, the Prophet lives amidst his companions and thus becomes a means of transmitting divine grace to the people.

90. The Kāba in Mecca is a cubical structure facing which the Muslims pray wherever they are. But if the worshipper is inside it, all directions become equally insignificant.

91. According to an alternative version, the line reads 'when will the sun and the moon unite?', which is reminiscent of the Quranic description of the Day of Judgement: 'When vision is dazzled, and the moon darkens, and the sun and the moon are joined.' (Surah 75: 7–9).

92. Gnosis or 'realization/recognition of the Truth' occurs often in Sufi literature.

93. For the story of Hīmāl and Nāgrāy, see note 22 under Vatsun above.

94. Bilāl was an Abyssinian slave who became a close companion of the Prophet of Islam. Tortured by the Meccan pagans for accepting Islam and devotion to the Prophet, he has come to symbolize values such as sacrifice, true devotion and Islam's egalitarian spirit.

95. Grit denotes the inner strength essential for the spiritual journey.

96. Here *dāl* written as ﺩ with its crooked shaped symbolizes servitude, whereas *alif* written as ﺍ is the first letter of the word Allah and symbolizes godhead and unity.

97. For some Sufis there is just the difference of one letter *meem* م between احد i.e., God and احمد, one of the names of the Prophet Muhammad. When the letter *hay* ح found a place between *alif* ا and *dal* د the word *ahad* احد came into existence. *Hay* is the intermediate between *alif* and *dal*, godhead and servitude, but all together constitute a single entity. The alphabetical symbolism invoked here suggests the idea of unity of being, discussed in the introduction.

98. Nooh in the Islamic tradition is the name of the Biblical Noah who is believed to have lived for a thousand years.

99. Ibrāhīm is the Biblical Abraham who in one the prophetic traditions is called *khalīlullah*, 'Allah's friend'.

100. Yusuf is Joseph, well known for his beauty.

101. Dāwood is David in Bible and known for his beautiful voice in which he used to sing the praise of God.

102. Sulaimān or Solomon the wise, was Dawood's son and enjoyed power over all animals and jinn. He also had wind under his command which he used to fly his throne.

103. Yahya is John the Baptist of the New Testament.

104. Moosa or Moses, according to the Quran, had a rare gift of conversing with God. Hence his epithet *kalīmullah*.

105. Luqmān, mentioned in the Quran, is believed to have been a sage.

106. According to a folklore tradition, Alexander tried to defeat death but failed.

107. Both Idrīs and Isa (Jesus) are prophets according to Islam. According to one tradition, they both were taken to the heavens alive.

108. Khizr or 'the green man' is the legendary immortal figure who remains hidden to the human eye and very rarely meets some chosen people to guide them.

109. The four closest companions of the Prophet, Abu Bakr, Umar, Uthman and Ali are also the first four caliphs of Islam.

110. According to some traditions, two angels named Nakīr and Munkar will question every person immediately after they are buried.

111. According to a verse in the Quran, the organs of the bodies of the sinners will testify against them on the day of judgement. 'And they will say to their skins, "Why bore you witness against us?" They shall say, "God gave us speech, as He gave everything speech. He created you the first time, and unto Him you shall be returned."' (Surah 41, verse 21).

112. A Quranic allusion. 'All that exists on earth will perish. And there will remain the face of your Lord, Owner of majesty and honour' (Surah 55, verse 27).

Masnavis

113. Gāmi follows the usual practice of Muslim poets, beginning with the praise of God and blessings on the Prophet Muhammad.

114. The first four caliphs of Islam.

115. Khusrau Parvaiz, the Sasanian ruler (r. 591–628), Shīrīn, the beautiful princess and Farhād, Khusrau's rival in love.

116. Anushīrwān was a famous king of ancient Persia.

117. Jamshīd, mythical king of Iran.

118. Two famous rulers of the ancient world.

119. The letter ghain غ has a dot on the top.

120. The black stone fitted in a wall of the Kāba in Mecca.

121. An allusion to the two teeth rows.

122. The letter *meem* ـﻤ in the Arabo–Persian script resembles the half of a curved arch with a round head.

123. Zamzam is a famous well near the Kāba in Mecca and sacred to the Muslims.

124. Hāroot and Māroot are two (fallen) angels according to tradition who were chained and imprisoned in a well in Babylon. The well was at the summit of the hill. Seekers of forbidden magical arts went there to be instructed by the fallen angels.

125. The Aleppo mirror was known for its high quality.

126. The literal meaning of Shīrīn is 'sweet'.

127. Her handmaidens are referred to as fairies and houries.

128. The famous lover of Yusuf in Islamic legend and literature.

129. Azra, the beloved of Vāmiq in a famous love story 'Vāmiq and Azra'.

130. If Shīrīn wants the permission of her family, Khusrau will ask for it.

131. Shīrīn compares herself with the midday lamp which is hardly noticed in the midday sun.

132. Parvaiz is Khusrau.

133. The two travails are separation from Shīrīn and the task.

134. Khusrau refers to himself as her kindred spirit.

135. Shīrīn would have preferred Khusrau killing her to his taking other women.

136. Meaning that fortune does not remain constantly good for anyone.

137. Shakar is already notorious for her inconstancy because she is a courtesan.

138. A pun on Shakar which means sugar.

139. Shīrīn boasts of her chastity.

140. Shīrīn evinces ambivalence in her affections for Farhād. Here, she dismisses Khusrau's charge that she ever thought of Farhād as her lover.

141. Pomegranates were believed to have medicinal properties and were hence often craved by the sick.

142. According to some reports, Malik Habibullah Shah was a rich person of Shahabad, Dooru. He could have been a patron of Gāmi.

143. *Safar* is the second month of the Muslim calendar.

144. 1199 of the Muslim calendar which corresponded with 1784 CE.

145. Shīrīn's giving and taking life both refer to her killing herself for Khusrau, her love.

146. Jāmi says that Zulaykha imagined him to be Potiphar of Egypt.

147. The beloved is sometimes addressed as the earring in Kashmiri poetry.

148. Yaqub (Jacob), the son of Ishāq (Isaac) was a Jewish prophet who had twelve sons, ten from a wife and Yusuf and his brother Benjamin from another. He loved Yusuf very dearly which evoked the jealousy of his half-brothers. They plan to get rid of him through treachery, begging their father to let Yusuf accompany them on a picnic. Once away, they thrash him, take off his shirt and throw him into a well. They then smear his shirt with an animal's blood and bring it to their father saying that a wolf devoured Yusuf.

149. Canaan in Palestine was Yaqub's homeland. Yusuf is often referred to as *māh-e kan'ān*, 'the moon of Canaan' in Persian, Urdu and Kashmiri poetry.

150. Gāmi often refers to the port of Surat which indicates that the port was famous for trade.

151. According to the Quran, Yusuf's half-brothers were filled with envy because they thought Yaqub was extremely fond of him and ignored them.

152. Jibrīl (Gabriel) is one of the four archangels in the Islamic belief system. He mainly serves as God's messenger to the prophets.

153. Khalīl is an epithet of Ibrāhīm (Abraham), a highly respected prophet in the Islamic and Judeo-Christian traditions.

154. Nooh (Noah) was an ancient prophet whose people denied him and were punished by God with a great flood. Nooh's flood finds mention in several verses of the Quran.

155. Several examples of hyperbole and personification are found in this passage.

156. The passage sums up the Sufi idea of Divine Beauty manifesting itself through the Creation.

157. See Introduction, p. xxvi–xxviii, for a discussion on the Divine Beauty manifesting itself through the creation.

158. Qibla is the direction facing which the Muslims say their prayers and namāz is the formal prayer offered five times a day.

159. See Introduction, p. xxvii–xxviii for explanation.

160. Rābia's transition from the love of form to essence finds a parallel in the Hindu girl in Sheikh San'ān's story.

161. The Beloved is God Himself.

162. The female lover uses hyperbolic terms such as 'young', 'ingenuous', 'naive' etc. in her expression of love.

163. 'Turk-like look'. The beloved is described as having a commanding appearance like a king or a warrior.

164. Cotton ball is a metaphor for the heart here.

165. Moon is another metaphor for the heart here.

166. When Yusuf refused to yield to Zulaykha's desire, she used her influence to send him to prison.

167. Here the reader gets an impression of hurriedness and lack of attention to some important strands of the narrative. Yusuf's stratagem is to retain his brother

Benjamin at his court in Egypt. Jāmi's *masnavi* omits the episodes related to Yusuf's half-brothers after his elevation as the de facto ruler of Egypt. Gāmi here takes the Quranic narrative as his source, according to which Yusuf's half-brothers arrive in Egypt in the time of severe famine to obtain provisions when they hear of his generosity. While they continue to think him a stranger, he immediately recognizes them. On inquiring about his brother Benjamin, they tell him that he is attending their father, now old and blind, but request Yusuf to give them his portion of the provisions too. Yusuf agrees but insists that they bring him along the next time otherwise they would not be entertained at his court. On their next visit, they bring Benjamin along. Yusuf takes him into confidence and through a stratagem retains him while others are allowed to go. He asks his servants to hide his own measuring cup in the luggage of Benjamin. When the brothers have left and travelled only a short distance, a cry is raised that Yusuf's cup is missing. Their belongings are searched and the cup retrieved from Benjamin's luggage. In keeping with the law, the thief has to become a bondsman of the man whose object he has stolen. This way Yusuf succeeds in having his long-lost brother near him. Gāmi omits all these details and, oddly, has Yusuf accuse Benjamin of theft when he is not even present at the court.

168. Gāmi here follows the convention of the Muslim poets like Attār and Jāmi who depict the experience of intense suffering in love as an eye-opener that enables the lovers to arrive at the right creed.

169. Expecting any good from you was like expecting to hold an elephant with a strand of hair.

170. This could be an allusion to the death of Gāmi's son Shah Sultan. See Introduction, p. xv.

171. The glad tiding that love confers immortality on true lovers and they do not die in the real sense.

172. An allusion to the Sufi concept of 'the light of Muhammad' (*noor-e Muhammadi*) which is believed to have been the first thing to be created and also through which the rest of the creation came into existence.

173. Here *jeem* written as ج has a horizontal line drawn over a semi-circle with a dot in the middle.

174. See note 150 for an explanation of the port of Surat.

175. Sayyid Amīr is Majnun's father.

176. Majnun describes his condition as that of a lion which has turned into a jackal, meaning that love has sucked all strength from him.

177. Majnun was beaten by street urchins and the people of Layla's tribe.

178. The separation from Majnun is like a serpent's sting for Sayyid Amīr.

179. *Herath* is Kashmiri for Shivarātri, a festival of Hindus.

180. The story of Sultan Mahmud Ghaznavi's love for his slave Ayāz is well known in Indo-Persian literature.

181. This oneness is not to be understood as physical intimacy but a spiritual one.

182. The Prophet Muhammad embodies the idea of oneness (*tawhīd*) as he is seen not merely as one among other prophets but the highest manifestation of the divine in the Sufi metaphysics. This, however, does not entail his divinity.

183. Another example of how the profane (*majāzi*) and divine (*haqīqi*) love are seen as different expressions of a single phenomenon. Just like Layla recognized her lover through the guise of a ram's skin, one must strive to recognize the unity behind diversity.

184. God, the Beloved, is only absent to the corporeal eye. He is very much near to those who can see beyond the apparent.

185. See note 22 under Vatsun for the Hīmāl and Nāgrāy legend. The allusion to the hair of the crown is especially telling because Hīmāl was left only with a tuft of Nāgrāy's hair when he was pulled into the underworld by his serpent-wives.

186. Gopal is an epithet of the Hindu god Krishna. Here Layla addresses Majnun just like a gopi (one of Krishna's female lovers) would have addressed him.

187. The dot of the letter *ghain* here denotes a blemish.

188. Like in many other instances, a shift occurs here and 'He' refers to the divine beloved, that is, God.

189. Reading the Quran together rehearses the act of their childhood in the school where their love first began.

190. This passage underscores the Sufi idea of the Word as the cause of all creation. The idea has its origin in the Quran according to which the Universe came into existence when God said, 'Be' (*kun*). 'He is the Originator of the heavens and the earth, and when He decrees something, He says only, "Be!" and it is.' (Surah 2, verse 117).

191. The King, i.e., God.

192. Majnun identifies with the fir tree completely, a state effected by the power of love.

193. 'Adept lover' (*pokhta kār*) is often used for a male lover who captures a woman's heart artfully.

194. *Fātiha* is the first chapter of the Quran, often recited over the dead.

195. An oft-repeated idea in Sufi poetry is that the Apparent and the Real are inextricably bound together. It is only through the Apparent that the Real can be known. In the context of this poem, it is the love between two

human beings which reflects its metaphysical and
hence real nature.

196. See note 195.

197. For a discussion on the Essence and the Attributes, see
Introduction, p. xxvi–xxvii and note 63 above.

198. Attār here is Fariduddin Attār, the author of *Mantiqut
Tayr*, Gāmi's source for this narrative.

199. The binary of faith and unfaith is transcended by the
power of love.

200. An allusion to the Quranic verses which some
Sufis interpret as describing how close the Prophet
Muhammad came to God during his night journey
to the Heaven. The verses read: 'Then he approached
and came closer. And was at a distance of but two
bow-lengths or even closer' (53: 8–9). For most
commentators, however, the verses describe how the
archangel Jibrīl came to the Prophet to deliver the
revelation. 'Two bow-lengths' in Sufi terminology is
used to state closeness.

201. Denigrating 'piety' in much of the Islamic poetry
is based on the idea of the primacy of love over the
observance of religious rules.

202. An allusion to her two braids hanging by two sides.

203. The Islamic proclamation of faith which says, 'There is
only one God and Muhammad is His messenger.'

204. An allusion to the Quranic verse: 'But those who
were blind in this world will be blind in the hereafter,
and most astray from the path' (17:72). The verse,
to be sure, is a general statement about those who
turn a blind eye to the truth when they see it, and
not about any particular people or section of the
humankind.

205. An allusion to the Muslim proclamation: 'There is no
god except God'.

206. An allusion to the Quranic verses about the martyrs who lay down their lives in the path of God. For Sufis, the greatest martyr is one who dies in the path of love. See 'The Moth's Tale', p. 46.

207. Mansur says he is *ahad* (the only one). See note 97 for the difference between *ahad* and *ahmad*.

208. *Jinn*, a species of invisible beings.

209. From the saying: 'A friend's flower hurts more than a foe's stone'.

210. Moosa, the famous Jewish prophet, also a prophet of Islam, frequently mentioned in the Quran.

211. According to the Jewish and Islamic traditions, God directly spoke to Moosa.

212. Those immersed in my love are like the drunk who do not follow the path meant for others.

213. The shepherd has now risen to a higher spiritual state and does not need to address God the way he did before. This way the divine law, which requires deference to a certain code of conduct, is given its due place in the story.

214. The lines from here to the end of the poem are adapted from the opening of Rumi's *Masnavi*, the celebrated 'Song of the Reed'.

215. An allusion to the Quranic story according to which Moosa asked God to let him have His glimpse. God agreed, provided Moosa can bear a tiny manifestation of God's self-disclosure on Mount Sinai, known as Mount Tūr in Islamic traditions. Moosa could not bear the vision and fell down unconscious (The Quran, Surah 7, verse 143).

Acknowledgements

Despite Mahmud Gāmi's great stature and unique place in the Kashmiri poetic tradition, he is one of its least translated poets. Exceptions to this are a few poems translated into English in the recent past and the famous Latin translation of his *masnavi* 'Yusuf Zulaykha' by Karl Friedrich Buckhardt, a German Orientalist, in the late nineteenth century. The present work offers, for the first time, a major portion of his collected works to the English reader. In addition to a substantial number of *vatsuns* and *nazms* (lyrical poems), it includes six of his major *masnavis* (narrative poems)—'Khusrau Shīrīn', Yusuf Zulaykha', 'Layla Majnun', 'Sheikh San'ān', 'Mansur's Tale' and 'The Shepherd's Tale'. This, therefore, is a moment of great satisfaction for me and an occasion to be thankful to all who have helped me in this endeavour.

First and foremost, I put on record my gratitude to the Indian Council of Philosophical Research, New Delhi, for sanctioning a major translation project on Mahmud Gāmi. The feedback of the Council's anonymous reviewer impelled me to undertake a thorough research into the philosophy of Sufi poetry that enabled me to write a comprehensive introduction to Gāmi. I also wish to thank Professor Shafi Shauq for helping me with the meaning of some archaic Kashmiri words and writing the foreword to this book.

Translating several hundred verses over a period of many months was a painstaking work carried out in seclusion and would not have been possible without my family's unwavering support. My deep gratitude is due to my wife Huma Galzie, son Mufti Khaleed, father Mufti Mearajuddin Farooqi, mother Mahmooda Mufti and brother Mufti Muzamil for their boundless love and for putting up with my studious habits. My parents-in-law, A.U. Khan and Mahmooda Ashai, have always been a great source of encouragement and love for which I want to thank them.

My colleagues in the Department of English, University of Kashmir, deserve a special mention. Nusrat Jan, Iffat Maqbool and Tasleem War have each provided a friendly and non-competitive working environment. I especially want to thank Iffat Maqbool for reading the introduction and offering valuable comments. Among my friends, I want to thank Inayat Rasool, Mearaj Bhat, Amir Suhail Wani, Faizan Bhat, Abid Ahmed and Maroof Shah. I also wish to thank the wonderful team at Penguin Random House for their meticulous work on the manuscript.

The translator's task, needless to say, is a difficult one. Trying to render accurately the meaning of the original in the target language and ensuring, simultaneously, that the translation is not dull or awkward or just readable but enjoyable too, is to negotiate a difficult terrain. I have tried my best to remain faithful to the original, conveying as much as possible its richness, complexity and mood into a modern English idiom. Notwithstanding this, I am fully aware that no translation is ever final. My hope is that this work will introduce Mahmud Gāmi to a wide readership and stimulate further interest in the rich tradition of Kashmiri poetry.

Mufti Mudasir Farooqi
Srinagar, Jammu and Kashmir
August 2022